THE HILDEG

M000284531

The Hildegard of Bingen Pilgrimage Book

Annette Esser

LITURGICAL PRESS
Collegeville, Minnesota

www.litpress.org

Cover design by Monica Bokinskie. Cover image: *Liber Scivias*. Prologue.

Map (cover and interior) © Naheland-Touristik GmbH Postfach 49 55606 Kirn.

Scripture quotations are from the New Revised Standard Version Bible © 1989 National Council of the Churches of Christ in the United States of America. Used by permission. All rights reserved worldwide.

Hildegard von Bingen <santa>, Liber divinorum operum, f., sec. XIII, State Library of Lucca, ms. 1942. Images used by permission of the Ministry of Culture - State Library of Lucca. Explicit prohibition of further reproductions or duplications by any means.

Images from the Scivias Codex used by permission of Klosterstiftung Sankt Hildegard, 65385 Rüdesheim am Rhein.

1   2   3   4   5   6   7   8   9

Library of Congress Cataloging-in-Publication Data

Names: Hildegard, Saint, 1098-1179. | Esser, Annette, editor, translator.
Title: The Hildegard of Bingen pilgrimage book / Annette Esser.
Other titles: Pilgerbuch. English
Description: Collegeville, Minnesota : Liturgical Press, 2022. | Includes
    bibliographical references. | Summary: "This book describes the ten
    stages of the Hildegard of Bingen Pilgrimage Way, a 140-kilometer
    path from Idar-Oberstein via Disibodenberg and Sponheim to
    St. Hildegard's Abbey in Eibingen on the Rhine. It also provides
    information about Hildegard's life and her theological, musical,
    medical, and botanic works, with accompanying biblical texts and
    meditative poems"— Provided by publisher.
Identifiers: LCCN 2022003932 (print) | LCCN 2022003933 (ebook) | ISBN
    9780814667651 (paperback) | ISBN 9780814667668 (epub) | ISBN
    9780814667668 (pdf)
Subjects: LCSH: Christian pilgrims and pilgrimages—Europe, Central.
    | Hildegard, Saint, 1098-1179. | BISAC: RELIGION / Christianity /
    Catholic | RELIGION / Christian Rituals & Practice / General
Classification: LCC BX2320.5.C36 P5513 2022 (print) | LCC BX2320.5.C36
    (ebook) | DDC 263/.04243—dc23/eng/20220325
LC record available at https://lccn.loc.gov/2022003932
LC ebook record available at https://lccn.loc.gov/2022003933

Contents

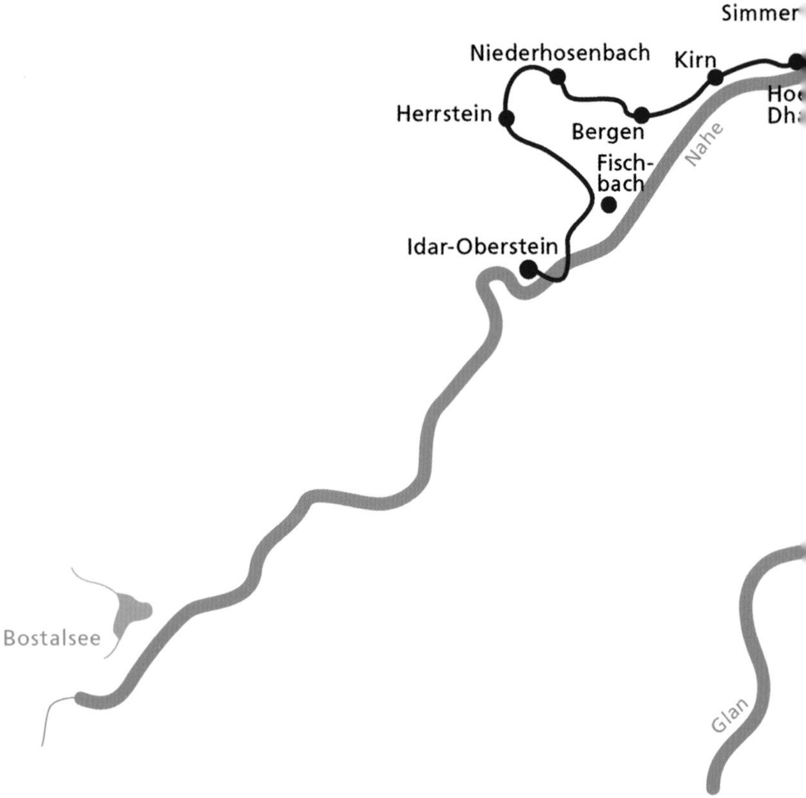

Simmer

Niederhosenbach

Kirn

Herrstein

Bergen

Hoe
Dha

Nahe

Fisch-
bach

Idar-Oberstein

Bostalsee

Glan

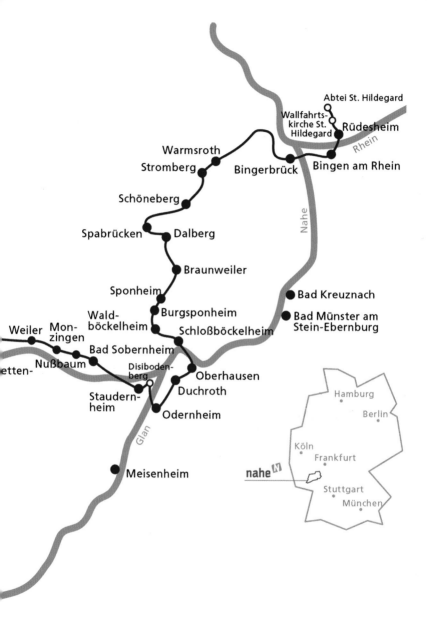

Abtei St. Hildegard

Wallfahrts-
kirche St.
Hildegard

Rüdesheim

Rhein

Warmsroth

Stromberg   Bingerbrück

Bingen am Rhein

Schöneberg

Nahe

Spabrücken   Dalberg

Braunweiler

Sponheim   Bad Kreuznach

Wald-   Burgsponheim   Bad Münster am
böckelheim   Stein-Ebernburg

Weiler   Mon-   Schloßböckelheim
          zingen

Bad Sobernheim

Nußbaum   Disiboden-
                         berg

etten-   Oberhausen

                         Duchroth
          Staudern-
          heim
                         Odernheim

Glan

Meisenheim

nahe [N]

Hamburg

Berlin

Köln   Frankfurt

Stuttgart

München

Foreword to the English Edition

Saint Hildegard of Bingen (1098–1179) has been called seeress, composer, physician, German prophetess. In 2012, she was promoted as Doctor of the Universal Church (*Doctor Ecclesiae Universalis*) by Pope Benedict XVI; she was only the fourth woman to receive this honor besides Catarina of Siena, Teresa of Ávila, and Thérèse of Lisieux. On September 9, 2017, the new Hildegard of Bingen Pilgrimage Route (*Hildegard von Bingen Pilgerwanderweg*) leading from Idar-Oberstein to Bingen on the Rhine was officially opened at the Disibodenberg, the very site where Hildegard lived for almost forty years of her life.

As a theologian and artist from Cologne, I have been studying and reflecting on Saint Hildegard for thirty years. At first, I translated Barbara Newman's groundbreaking monography, *Sister of Wisdom: Saint Hildegard's Theology of the Feminine*, from English into German. In 2009, I founded the Scivias Institute for Art and Spirituality, a nonprofit organization. Yet, it was only in 2014, after my own pilgrimage on the Camino de Santiago in Spain, that I initiated the creation of the Hildegard Pilgrimage Way in the historic land where Hildegard lived in the twelfth century (and where I live and work today). This was possible because—as a newly elected member of the local District Parliament of Bad Kreuznach—I found strong supporters for this project: at first Bettina Dickes, who is today the head of the district authority; then also the tourist organization for the Naheland region (Naheland-Touristik) that gave this project a top priority and managed to get it financially supported by the European Union.

As a European project, the Hildegard Way has a European domain name (www.hildegardweg.eu) and all texts of the 59 tableaux on the 140-kilometer Hildegard Way are in German and English.

Longing for the Sun of Justice by Annette Esser, oil and gold on canvas, 50 x 40 cm, 2017

The concept of these tableaux was developed by me and written by a team of authors facilitated by the Scivias Institute, including sisters of St. Hildegard Abbey: of these, 27 meditation tableaux follow Hildegard's major mystical work, *Liber Scivias*,[1] and 31 information tableaux present Hildegard's medical, musical, and ethical works, and the historical sites where the saint lived. In 2017, I compiled the pilgrimage book in German (*Pilgerbuch. Hildegard von Bingen Pilgerwanderweg*, Verlag Matthias Ess, Bad Kreuznach, 2017 and 2019); this book was designed with many pictures in a wonderful color concept by graphic designer Sandra Ess. Following up in 2019, I undertook the first English translation of *The Hildegard of Bingen Pilgrimage Book*. I am grateful that this book was carefully proofread by Drs. Ruth Griffoen, Beverly Kienzle, and Debra Stoudt; that the German publisher released the book and graphic design for free; and that the American publisher, Liturgical Press, carried out the English edition with much expertise and engagement.

This book contains the complete texts of the 59 tableaux as well as images, stories, and poems. The visionary images are from Hildegard's mystical work *Liber Scivias* and from her *Liber Divinorum Operum*. Additionally, there are photos from the "land of Hildegard," the region in today's Rhineland-Palatine where Hildegard lived. Also included are some of Hildegard's songs as well as new poems about Hildegard by Karen S. E. Stock from Canada, Colleen Keating from Australia, and some of my own poems and artworks. And each "Text of the Day" tells the story of Hildegard's life, her visions and visionary theology, her original notion of *viriditas*—the green power of life—and the story of the Abbey (by Sr. Philippa Rath, OSB).

I think I speak for all of us, who have worked hard and with much enthusiasm on realizing this project, when I now say: Welcome to a visit to the land of Hildegard. Welcome to a Hildegard Pilgrimage! In Saint Hildegard's words:

o quam mirabilis—how wonderful!

Annette Esser, Bad Kreuznach, Germany,
March 2022

STAGE 1

Idar-Oberstein – Herrstein

1

Idar-Oberstein – Herrstein

Length 20.5 km – ca. 7 hrs. – Ascent 815 m – Descent 756 m – difficult

The first stage of the Hildegard Way starts in Idar-Oberstein. On the pedestrian path to the Church in the Rock (*Felsenkirche*), you find the first meditation tableau; it shows Hildegard, the seeress (**Tableau 1**).

Internationally, Idar-Oberstein is the town of gemstones and lapidaries. Thus, various museums depict the history of mining and glyptic art in this region and invite you to admire the precious jewels that have been gathered here from all over the world. Fittingly, the first information tableau is positioned at the German Mineral Museum (Deutsches Mineralienmuseum) and concerns Hildegard's book on stones (**Tableau 2**). The abbess, who practiced the art of healing, did not write about stones as such but about their healing effects on people.

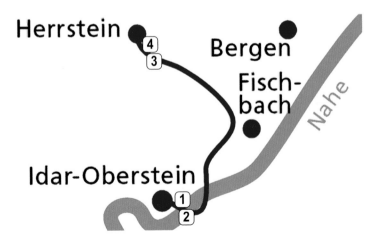

View of the Hunsrück mountain range to Herrstein

The stage then leads from the Nahe Valley into the Hunsrück mountain range. Due to the natural difficulty of this section, the long path to Herrstein is now divided into two parts. The first part (1A) leads from the Church in the Rock east beyond the Nahe Valley to a site near Fischbach. There, one may stay overnight and then walk the second part to Herrstein (1B) on the next day. For pilgrims whose time is limited or who may find the long ascent too challenging, we recommend driving part of this way to Herrstein.

Church in the Rock (*Felsenkirche*) in Idar-Oberstein

The next meditation tableau is located in front of the old Protestant Castle Church (*Schlosskirche*) in Herrstein (**Tableau 3** "God Enthroned") and the information tableau in the historic center presents the history of the County of Sponheim since the Middle Ages (**Tableau 4**).

TABLEAU 1

The Seeress

Church in the Rock, Idar-Oberstein

Liber Scivias. Prologue

PILGRIM'S REFLECTION

What do I know and what do I think about
Hildegard of Bingen (1098–1179)?

Why do I want to go on a pilgrimage on
the Hildegard Way?

THE SEERESS

"And behold! In the forty-third year of my earthly course, as I was gazing with great fear and trembling attention at a heavenly vision, I saw a great splendor in which resounded a voice from Heaven, saying to me, 'O fragile human, ashes to ashes, and filth of filth! Say and write what you see and hear.'"

Hildegard of Bingen

The first illumination from the prologue of *Liber Scivias* shows Hildegard receiving the "living light" from heaven above, which flows in five fiery tongues from the roof of a building. On her lap is a wax tablet on which she writes down what she receives. To the right, the monk Volmar looks at her from an aisle. He holds a piece of paper or parchment onto which he will finally write down what the seeress dictates to him. This will become Hildegard's first book, whose title is also a calling: *Scivias—Know the ways.*

I was in the Spirit on the Lord's day, and I heard behind me a loud voice like a trumpet saying, "Write in a book what you see and send it to the seven churches."

Revelation 1:10-11

SONG

O splendissima gemma

O splendissima gemma
et serenum decus solis,

qui tibi infusus est,
fons saliens de corde Patris,

qui est unicum Verbum suum,
per quod creavit
mundi primam materiam,
quam Eva turbavit.

Hoc Verbum effabricavit tibi,
Pater, hominem,
et ob hoc es tu illa lucida
materia,
per quam hoc ipsum Verbum
exspiravit
omnes virtutes,
ut exudit in prima materia
omnes creaturas.

O resplendent jewel
and unclouded beauty of
the sun
poured into you:
a fountain springing from the
Father's heart.
This is the only Word,
by which he created
the primal matter
which Eve threw into Chaos.

For you, the Father fashioned
this word into a man.
So you are the luminous
matter
through which the Word
breathed forth
all virtues,
as in the primal matter
he brought forth all creatures.

Hildegard of Bingen[1]

TABLEAU 2

Stones

Deutsches Mineralienmuseum, Idar-Oberstein

Liber Physica 4

Emerald – Jacinth – Onyx – Beryl – Sardonyx – Sapphire –
Sard – Topaz – Chrysolith – Jasper – Prasine – Chalcedony –
Chrysoprase – Carbuncle – Amethyst – Agate – Diamond –
Magnesian Stone – Ligure – Chrystal – Pearls – Mother-of-Pearl –
Carnelian – Alabaster – Limestone – Glass – and other stones.

In this region that is enriched by gemstones, Hildegard
of Bingen (1098–1179) lived between Niederhosenbach, the
Disibodenberg and Bingen. So, her teaching of the stones belongs to the Hildegard Way. We find it in the fourth book of
her *Physica*. According to her cosmic vision, stones and gems
were created in the first two days of creation; there already
was gold, bdellium and onyx in the garden of Paradise (Gen
2:12). Gemstones are also important in the history of Israel
(Exod 28:16-20; 39:10-15). Finally, twelve jewels will build up
the foundation of the heavenly Jerusalem (Rev 21:14-21). Hildegard was convinced that certain gems can support healing
in various afflictions and she describes in detail the healing
effects of twenty-six (gem-) stones. *"Every stone contains fire and
moisture. The devil abhors, detests and disdains precious stones."*

The emerald (smaragdus) *grows in the wee hours of morning at sunrise, when the sun is powerfully placed in its orbit, traversing its route.
Then the natural vigor of the earth and grasses is especially lively. . . .
One who has great pain in his/her head should hold it near his/her mouth
and warm it by one's breath. . . . The warm humidity of the breath of
the soul will induce the green power and the effect of the stone.*

Sapphire (sapphirus) *is hot and develops at noontime, when the sun burns ardently and the air is a bit obstructed by its heat. . . . If this stone is placed on a ring of the purest gold, without tin . . . then a person may place the stone in his mouth as medicine.*

Jasper (jaspis) *develops when the sun is beginning to set, after the ninth hour of the day, and it is warmed by the fire of the sun. . . . When a person wants to consider and deal with an issue on which he/she has spent much carefulness and affection . . . he/she shall put a jasper in one's mouth and the power of the stone permeates the capability and the reason of this person and it will strengthen and hold his/her spirit.*

Amethyst (amethystus) *develops when the sun shows its circle . . . which it does when it prefigures some change. . . . The serpent and adder flee this stone.*

Agate (achates) *is born from certain sand of water which extends from the east to the south. It is hot and fiery. . . . If someone carries an agate with him/her, he/she should place it next to one's bare skin, thus warming it. Its nature will make this person capable, judicious, and prudent in speech, because it is born from fire and air and water. . . . Some precious stones placed on one's skin, make him/her healthy and sensible by one's virtue.*

> The foundations of the wall of the city are adorned with every jewel; the first was jasper, the second sapphire, the third agate, the fourth emerald, the fifth onyx, the sixth carnelian, the seventh chrysolite, the eighth beryl, the ninth topaz, the tenth chrysoprase, the eleventh jacinth, the twelfth amethyst. And the twelve gates are twelve pearls, each of the gates is a single pearl, and the street of the city is pure gold, transparent as glass.
>
> Revelation 21:19-21

TABLEAU 3

God Enthroned

Schlosskirche, Herrstein

Liber Scivias I.1

PILGRIM'S REFLECTION

What image do I have of God?

What kind of position and attitude do I have towards God?

"I saw a great mountain the color of iron, and enthroned on it One of such great glory that it blinded my sight."

Hildegard of Bingen

In the first vision of the first book of *Scivias,* **Hildegard sees God as the winged One enthroned on a mountain. Below, in front of the mountain, there are two female figures. To the left, covered all over with eyes, is** *Timor Dei,* **the fear of God.** With her whole consciousness, she is aware and she observes the will of God. **To the right is** *Paupertas,* **the poor one in spirit**. Above her head such an abundance of divine light is outpouring that one cannot see her face anymore; she appears headless, so to speak, in the miniature. That means that she **lives from the ray of light and is utterly connected with it.**

Thus, at the beginning of her major mystical work *"Scivias—Know the Ways"* Hildegard invites us to contemplate the necessary attitude of the human being towards God. The two female figures show the female attitude of receiving and surrender, that is the basic mystical attitude. Thus, Mary's words to the angel, her *Fiat voluntas tua*—"let it be with me according to your word" (Luke 1:38), express the virginal attitude of receiving. In her spiritual women's stories, Petra Urban, a contemporary writer from Bingen, has spelled out the positive value of this experience of surrender and even headlessness:

> Sometimes it can be good that we take this Mary as our model. That is, to consistently leave our hands off daily routine in certain moments of our lives, to forget about all obligations for a moment, and instead to dive into the depth of our being and to feel the presence of God. Not thinking, not wanting anything. Only feeling. Only being . . . faithfully being thoughtless. Being headless, in the best sense of the

word. . . . Suddenly, something happens within us. A sort of power opens up. It is as if the world around us is shining in a special light from one moment to the next. This is a light that connects everything with everything. Nothing seems to exist for itself anymore, everything points to something else. To completeness. And we, as we sit and marvel and feel the flow of the divine and the holiness deep inside of us, we experience ourselves as part of this completeness. For suddenly we are as light as laughter, broad as the air that covers us, and transparent for all vibrations around us. We are tree and leaf and light and birdsong, we are the rustle of the wind and the silence at the same time, the fragrance of the blossoms, the humming of the bees, sky and clouds and the warm smell of the earth, as well as everything else. In short: We are fullness, nothing but fullness in this moment. We are life. We are divine, complete being.[2]

So, at the beginning of Hildegard's *Scivias* and at the beginning of the pilgrimage, everything depends on this: we need to let go of the many thoughts that we are preoccupied with in our daily life; we need to get empty in order to be capable and ready to receive something new.

Blessed are the poor in spirit, for theirs is the kingdom of heaven.
Blessed are those who mourn, for they will be comforted.
Blessed are the meek, for they will inherit the earth.
Blessed are those who hunger and thirst for righteousness, for they will be filled.
Blessed are the merciful, for they will receive mercy.
Blessed are the pure in heart, for they will see God.

Matthew 5:3-8

TABLEAU 4

The County of Sponheim

Schlosskirche, Herrstein

The town of Herrstein originated in the thirteenth century as a settlement around *Herestyn* castle. Today's *Schlosskirche* derives from the old Castle Church. The castle belonged to the earls of Sponheim (*Spanheim*). As legend tells us, the German word *Span* (English: splint) marked them as Christian knights who were honored to own a splinter of the Holy Cross. During the lifetime of Hildegard of Bingen (1098–1179), the county of Sponheim began to develop as an important territory within the Holy Roman Empire; it existed until the French Revolution. Hildegard's teacher, Jutta of Sponheim (1092–1136) was the sister of Meinhard of Sponheim (1085–1135) who named himself as the first Earl of Sponheim. The foundation of more than twenty castles and towns secured the sphere of control. Kreuznach, Enkirch, Kastellaun and Trarbach were especially important towns economically and militarily. The citizens enjoyed freedom from bondage and feudal government. Even though they had to pay a tribute to the town's Lord and perform certain tasks, for example building and maintaining the city wall, they could regulate many things on their own. The special purpose of the town's foundation (after 1260) was the protection of the Niederwörresbach and Niederhosenbach settlements. The latter is now considered the most likely birthplace of Hildegard of Bingen, according to recent historical research (cf. **Tableau 6**).

Michael Vesper

Sepulchral stele in Marian Chapel at Disibodenberg

First Station
in Hildegard's Life:
Childhood and Visionary Gift

by Annette Esser

In the spring of 1098 AD,[3] a girl was born at a manor house in the midst of the Holy Roman Empire.[4] The noble parents Hildebert and Mechthild named their tenth child Hildegard, and, "while sighing," they dedicated her to God as a tithe. Such a dedication of a newborn child by parents was not unusual in her time. Later in her life, Hildegard accepted it for herself, though she did not recommend the practice to others. Seven of Hildegard's nine older siblings are known to us: the three brothers Drutwin (the oldest brother and therefore the heir), Roricus (later a cantor at Mainz Cathedral) and Hugo (later a canon in Tholey), and her four sisters, Irmgard, Jutta, Odila and Clementia, one of whom later took the veil in Hildegard's convent. In other words, four of the children chose a religious life. This also was not as unusual in her time as it seems today.

Up to the age of eight Hildegard grew up as an often sickly child in the family manor house, surrounded by her siblings, protected and cared for as well as was possible in her time. Of course, her parents had men and women servants who worked for them at their manor. On the surrounding leasehold lands, the serfs were required to give a tithe of their harvest to the landlord. At the time, the nobility was considered to be endowed by God with special qualities and abilities, and they did not have to do agricultural work on their own farmland. A nobleman was free (*liberatus*), which also meant free to study the "liberal arts." Of course, this was only possible for men (*Freiherren*), not for women. Hildegard deeply internalized this aristocratic and hierarchical thinking and defended it throughout her life, even against criticism from the monastic reform movement.[5]

The twelfth century was a tumultuous time and Hildegard's family did not live at the edges of the Holy Roman Empire but rather in the center. The imperial palace at Ingelheim was located nearby. The ships on the Rhine brought goods and news from all over the world, from Scandinavia to Italy and from Spain to Jerusalem. Her family had good contacts in the "golden" city of Mainz:

> *Hildegard's father probably rode often . . . to Mainz, the seat of the Archbishop. Perhaps he brought a fine suit of armor from there, because at that time Mainz armor was so popular that it was traded as far away as London. For their mother, he may have brought expensive fabrics from the market, and, for the kitchen, he brought spices from distant lands. Back at the manor, the family listened as Hildebert of Bermersheim spoke about the town by the river, of the mighty walls behind which loomed the towers of magnificent churches that protected huge stone buildings, vineyards and orchards.*[6]

In the Holy Roman Empire, which contained a mere seventeen fortified cities, the old Roman bishopric of Mainz was called the "diadem of the empire." Together with the other major bishopric, the city of Cologne, whose city walls had just been expanded in a semi-circular form in 1106, and with Regensburg, it was one of the three leading political and economic centers. For this reason, this aristocratic family was probably always well informed about what was happening in the Holy Roman Empire: the First Crusade to the Holy Land (1096), the persecution and killing of Jews in Speyer and Mainz (1096), the escape (1099) and return of Ruthard, Archbishop of Mainz (1105), and, the overthrow of King Henry IV by his own son Henry V (1104) and his captivity in the nearby Castle of Böckelheim (1105). All of this was certainly the subject of conversation at the manor. In any case, there was always "something going on," much work, but also play and feasts.

In her later autobiographical writing, Hildegard herself reported nothing about all these external and historical events of her life. She mentioned only the year 1100, which she understood as a turning point to an "effeminate age" (*muliebre tempus*). Apparently, looking back at her life, she regarded something completely different to be important to her, namely her own inner experience:

> When I was first fashioned, when in my mother's womb God raised me up with the breath of life, he impressed this vision in my soul. For by the one thousand and one hundredth year after the Incarnation of Christ, the teaching of the Apostles and the burning righteousness which he had established in Christians and in the spiritual, began to slacken and turn to wavering. It was in those times I was born, and my parents, with sighs, promised me to God. In my third year of age I saw so great a light that my soul trembled, but, because I was still an infant, I count not convey anything about it.
>
> In my eighth year I was offered to God for a spiritual way of life, and until my fifteenth year I used to see many things and often spoke about them in my simplicity, so that those who heard them wondered where they might be coming from and from whom. Then I too wondered at it in myself, that while I beheld these things inwardly in my soul, I yet had my outward sight as well, and I did not hear this of anyone else. So I concealed the vision I saw in my soul for as long as I could, and was ignorant of many outward events because of a recurring ailment I have suffered from my mother's milk until now, which wore out my flesh and sapped my strength.[7]

Only much later in her life, at the age of seventy-nine, was Hildegard willing to describe her visionary experience in more detail. This is found in her letter to the Flemish monk Guibert of Gembloux:

From my early childhood, before my bones, nerves, and veins were fully strengthened, I have always seen this vision in my soul, even to the present time, when I am more than seventy years old. In this vision my soul, as God would have it, rises up high into the vault of heaven and into the changing sky and spreads itself out among different people, although they are far away from me in distant lands and places. And because I see them in this way in my soul, I observe them in accord with the shifting clouds and other created things. I do not hear them with my outward ears, nor do I perceive them by the thought of my heart or by any combination of my five senses, but in my soul alone, while my outward eyes are open. So I have never fallen prey to ecstasy in the visions, but I see them wide awake, day and night. . . .

The light that I see thus is not spatial, but it is far, far brighter than a cloud that carries the sun. I can measure neither height, nor length, nor breadth in it; and I call it "the reflection of the living light." And as the sun, the moon, and the stars appear in water, so writings, sermons, virtues, and certain human actions take form for me and gleam within it.

Now whatever I have seen or learned in this vision remains in my memory for a long time, so that, when I have seen and heard it, I remember; and I see, hear and know all at once, and as if in an instant I learn what I know. . . .

Moreover, I can no more recognize the form of this light than I can gaze directly on the sphere of the sun. Sometimes—but not often—I see within this light another light, which I call "the living Light." And I cannot describe when and how I see it, but while I see it all sorrow and anguish leave me, so that then I feel like a simple girl instead of an old woman.[8]

STAGE 2

Herrstein –
Niederhosenbach –
Bergen –
Kirn

2

Herrstein – Niederhosenbach – Bergen – Kirn

Length 15.6 km – ca. 4.5 hrs. – Ascent 276 m – Descent 400 m

The second stage guides us from medieval Herrstein to the village of Niederhosenbach. According to recent historical research, Hildegard was born here; her descent from a noble family is the theme of the information tableau (**Tableau 6**). Thanks to the former pastor, the small Protestant church houses a facsimile edition of *Scivias*—Hildegard's major mystical work that brought her fame. As we follow the order of Hildegard's visions on the Hildegard Way, we are presented next with a meditation tableau on her second vision, "Creation and the Fall" (**Tableau 5**). In front of the church there is an old oak tree and a meditation place that invites the pilgrim to rest.

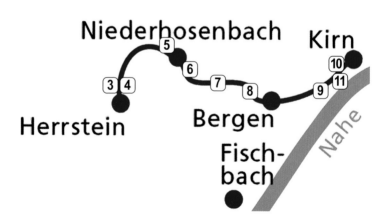

The medieval town of Herrstein

From Niederhosenbach, the Hildegard Way leads further to Bergen. In the forest area, there is an information tableau on Hildegard's Book of Trees (**Tableau 7**). In Bergen, Italian-speaking former Reverend Paul Krachen set up the guesthouse "Toscana im Hunsrück," where he cooks Italian food, and which is now also a Hildegard station for pilgrims. You can at least get some water here and reflect on the meditation tableau "The Cosmos" (**Tableau 8**).

The way from Bergen continues on its course to Kirn, thereby passing along the Trübenbachtal brook valley. On a hillside, the next tableau informs about Hildegard's Book of Birds (**Tableau 9**).

In the evening, the tired pilgrim deserves a Kirn beer, thus acting on Hildegard's advice "One shall drink beer!" (**Tableau 10**).

The Protestant church of Niederhosenbach

Facsimile of the *Liber Scivias* in the church of Niederhosenbach

For the reading of the day, we recommend the article about Hildegard's visionary experience and visionary book, *Scivias*, which we are following on this whole pilgrimage way.

Kirn marketplace

O quam mirabilis

O quam mirabilis est
praescientia divini pectoris
quae praescivit
omnem creaturam.

O how marvelous is
the foreknowledge
of the heart of God,
that foreknew all creation.

Nam cum Deus inspexit
faciem hominis quem formavit,

For when God looked
on the face of the man he
     had formed,

omnia opera sua
in eadem forma hominis
integra aspexit.

he saw all this works whole
in the form of that man.

O quam mirabilis est
*   inspiration,*
quae hominem sic suscitavit.

O how marvelous is the
     breath of the Spirit
that roused man to life!

Hildegard of Bingen[1]

TABLEAU 5

Creation and the Fall

Niederhosenbach Protestant Church

Liber Scivias I.2

PILGRIM'S REFLECTION

What do I think about the origin of
good and evil?

_____

_____

_____

_____

_____

_____

_____

_____

_____

_____

_____

_____

_____

_____

"Then I saw as it were a great multitude of very bright living lamps, which received fiery brilliance and acquired an unclouded splendor. And behold! A pit of great breadth and depth appeared, with a mouth like the mouth of a well, emitting fiery smoke with great stench, from which a loathsome cloud spread out and touched a deceitful, vein-shaped form. And, in a region of brightness, it blew upon a white cloud that had come forth from a beautiful human form and contained within itself many and many stars, and so doing, cast out both the white cloud and the human form from that region. When this was done, a luminous splendor surrounded that region, and all the elements of the world, which before had existed in great calm, were turned to the greatest agitation and displayed horrible terrors."*

In the second vision of the first book of *Scivias*, Hildegard looks at the beginning of creation. There, in the image below, she sees the two trees of life and of knowledge. Above them in a horizontal position is Adam, the first human being. With his right ear, he is listening to a fire that comes from a dark kind of figure to the left; this figure symbolizes the dark and evil side in us and amongst us. It is stretching to the heavenly spheres above like a tree from which a head of a serpent grows like a branch. This head touches a green cloud coming from Adam's side. This cloud represents Eve, the "mother of all living" (Gen 3:20). She bears in her womb all future generations as stars. Thus, just as she is touched by the "evil serpent," also all the sons and daughters of Eve, meaning all of us human beings, are endangered by evil.

Then the LORD God formed the man [Adam] from the dust of the ground, and breathed into his nostrils the breath of life; and the man became a living being. . . .

So the LORD God caused a deep sleep to fall upon the man, and he slept; then he took one of his ribs and closed up its place with flesh. And the rib that the LORD God had taken from the man he made into a woman and brought her to the man. . . .

And the man and his wife were both naked, and were not ashamed. . . . Now the serpent was more crafty than any other wild animal that the LORD God had made. He said to the woman, "Did God say, 'You shall not eat from any tree in the garden'?" . . .

So when the woman saw that the tree was good for food, and that it was a delight to the eyes, and that the tree was to be desired to make one wise, she took of its fruit and ate; and she also gave some to her husband, who was with her, and he ate. Then the eyes of both were opened, and they knew that they were naked. . . .

But the LORD God called to the man, and said to him, "Where are you?". . .

Then the LORD God said to the woman, "What is this that you have done?"

The LORD God said to the serpent,
    "Because you have done this,
        cursed are you among all animals
        and among all wild creatures;
    upon your belly you shall go,
        and dust you shall eat
        all the days of your life.
    I will put enmity between you and the woman,
        and between your offspring and hers." . . .

The man named his wife Eve [life], because she was the mother of all living. And the LORD God made garments of skins for the man and for his wife, and clothed them. Then the LORD God said, "See, the man has become like one of us, knowing good and evil; and now, he might reach out his hand and take also of the tree of life, and eat, and live forever"— therefore the LORD God sent him forth from the garden of Eden, to till the ground from which he was taken. He drove out the man; and at the east of the garden of Eden he placed the cherubim, and a sword flaming and turning to guard the way to the tree of life.

Genesis 2:7, 21-22, 25; 3:1, 6-7, 9, 13-15, 20-24

TABLEAU 6

Hildegard's Origin

Niederhosenbach Protestant Church

View of Niederhosenbach

"In the Holy Roman Empire, during the reign of Henry IV, a virgin lived in this side of Gaul; famous by the nobility of her descent and by her holiness, she had the name Hildegard, daughter of father Hildebert and mother Mechtild."

Vita Sanctae Hildegardis

From Hildegard's *Vita*, we learn that she was of noble descent and that her homeland is Gaul on the Western side of the Rhine. The oldest specification about the place of her birth is by Trithemius of Sponheim (1462–1516) who identifies it as the castle of Böckelheim. The newer research by Sr. Marianna Schrader (1942) has assumed the village of Bermersheim near Alzey, and, the most recent historical research by Josef Heinzelmann proposes that Hildegard was born in Niederhosenbach. This is because Hildebert was presumably Lord of Bermersheim and Niederhosenbach and descended from an old noble family. It is not yet clear whether Hildegard was related to Jutta of Sponheim, to whom she came at the age of eight. In any case, the family lived in a manor house, probably had bondservants and was provided by the surrounding leasehold land with the tithe. According to her *Vita*, she was the tenth of ten children (Drutwin, Roricus, Irmgard, Jutta, Odila and Clementia are named) and she grew up being well-looked after and taken care of as much as was possible in her time. Throughout her life, her noble descent was the base of her distinctive class consciousness, thereby building an important precondition for her successful work.

TABLEAU 7

Trees

On the Way to Bergen

Liber Divinorum Operum I.4

Nutmeg – Frankincense – Myrrh – Balsam – Aloe –
Brechit – Apple Tree – Pear Tree – Walnut Tree – Quince Tree –
Peach Tree – Cherry Tree – Plum Tree – Rowan – Black Mulberry –
Almond Tree – Hazel Tree – Chestnut Tree – Medlar Tree –
Fig Tree – Laurel Tree – Olive Tree – Date Palm – Citron Tree –
Cedar Tree – Cypress – Savin – Box Tree – Fir Tree – Linden –
Oak – Beech Tree – Ash Tree – Aspen – Alder Tree – Maple Tree –
Yew Tree – White Birch – Sea Fir – Spindle Tree – English Elm –
Willow – Sallow – Folbaum – Silver Willow – Cornel Cherry Tree –
Field Maple – Sweet Gale – Juniper – Elder – Barberry Tree –
Hartrogelbaum (dogwood) – Elm – Black Cherry – Privet –
Genista – Hawthorn – Dog Rose – Sloe – Vine –
Gichtbaum / Black currant – Smoke – Moss

Hildegard lived in the spacious forest region of Central Europe, where, in her time of the twelfth century, the primeval forests were largely cleared. Her treatise about fifty-eight regional and exotic trees and bushes, including resins, spices and mosses, in the third book of *Physica*, complements the extensive theme of healing plants of the first book. According to Hildegard, not only fruits, leaves and roots, but also the wood and ashes as well as the surrounding earth of the trees may have healing or harmful effects on the human being. She also connects trees with certain characteristics, virtues and vices of the human being. She writes: *"All trees have either heat or cold in them."*

The apple tree (affaldra) *is hot and moist and it is of such great moisture that it would even flow forth, if not constrained by the heat. . . . The fruit of this tree is gentle and easily digested. . . . They are good for healthy people to eat raw, since they are ripened by the strong dew. . . . But cooked or dried apples are good for both sick and healthy people.*

The quince tree (quittenbaum) *is very cold and of subtlety which is assimilated, sometimes usefully, other times not. . . . Its fruit is hot* and dry and has a good balance in it. When it is ripe and eaten raw, it harms neither a sick nor a healthy person. It is very useful, cooked and roasted, for a sick or healthy person to eat.

The almond tree (*amygdalus*) is very hot and has a bit of moisture in it. Its bark, leaves, and sap are not much use as medicine, because all its power is in the fruit. One whose brain is empty, and whose face has a bad color from a pain in the head, should frequently eat the inmost kernels of this fruit. They fill his brain and give him the correct color.

The chestnut tree (*kestenbaum*) is very hot but has great power mixed with that heat. . . . The virtue in it, and its fruit, is useful against all infirmity in a human. . . . For one who ails in the stomach, boil these kernels in water and bread crumbs in a small dish. Add powdered licorice, and a little powder from the root of the female fern to the mixture, and cook them again with the chestnuts, to prepare a mush. When the person eats this, it will purge his stomach and make it warm and strong.

The beech tree (*boiche, fagus*) has correct balance, with heat and cold, both of which is good. It denotes discipline.

SONG

O virtus Sapientiae

O virtus Sapientiae,
quae circuiens circuisti
comprehendo omnia
in una via,
quae habet vitam,
tres alas habens,
quarum una in altum volat
et altera de terra sudat
et tertia undique volat.
   everywhere.

O power of Wisdom!
You encompassed the cosmos,
encircling and embracing all
in one living orbit

with your three wings:
one soars on high,
one distills the earth essence,
and the third hovers

Laus tibi sit,
sicut te decet,
O Sapientia.

Praise to you,
Wisdom,
fitting praise!

Hildegard of Bingen[2]

TABLEAU 8

The Cosmos

Bergen

Liber Scivias I.3

PILGRIM'S REFLECTION

How do I imagine the cosmos?

What is the position of human beings in the cosmos?

Where is God?

THE COSMOS

*"After this I saw a vast instrument, round and shadowed, in the shape of an **egg**, small at the top, large in the middle and narrowed at the bottom; outside it, surrounding its circumference, there was **bright fire** with, as it were, a **shadow zone** under it. And in that fire there was **a globe of sparkling flame** so great that the whole instrument was illuminated by it, over which **three torches** were arranged. . . . But from the fire that surrounded the instrument issued **a blast with whirlwinds**, and from the zone beneath it rushed forth another blast with whirlwinds, and from the zone, too, there was a **dark fire** of such great horror that I could not look at it, whose force shook the whole zone, full of thunder, tempest and exceeding sharp stones both large and small. . . . But beneath that zone was purest ether, with no zone beneath it, and in it I saw **a globe of white fire** and great magnitude over which **two little torches** were placed. . . . And in that ether were scattered many bright spheres. . . . And from that ether too **blast** came forth with its whirlwinds. . . . And beneath that ether I saw **watery air** with a white zone beneath it, which diffused itself here and there and imparted moisture to the whole instrument. . . . And in the midst of these elements was a **sandy globe** of great magnitude. . . . And I saw between the North and the East a great mountain, which to the North had great darkness and to the East had great light."*

Hildegard of Bingen

In this wonderful third vision of the first book of *Scivias*, we see Hildegard's holistic view of the cosmos, of the forces that influence the human being and of God.

In the following commentary, the "voice from heaven" interprets the single elements of her cosmic vision:

Instrument in the shape of an egg
Almighty God

Bright fire
Fire of God's comfort

Shadow zone / dark fire
The fire of revenge: noisiness, fratricide

Globe of white fire
The invincible church

Four winds
  1. **Wind from the South**
     True knowledge by proper proclamation
  2. **Wind from the North**
     Satanic fury
  3. **Wind from the East**
     True and perfect teaching
  4. **Wind from the West**
     Proclamation of truth by the strongest sermons

Watery air
Bath of baptism

Sandy globe
"This openly shows that, of all strengths of God's creation, Man's is most profound, made in a wondrous way with great glory from the dust of the earth and so entangled with the strength of the rest of creation that he can never be separated from them."

Great mountain
The tension between the light in the East and the darkness in the North shows the deep fall between divine grace and devilish godlessness.

In the beginning when God created the heavens and the earth, the earth was a formless void and darkness covered the face of the deep, while a wind from God swept over the face of the waters.

Genesis 1:1-2

Bless the LORD, O my soul.
O LORD my God, you are
very great.
You are clothed with honor
and majesty,
wrapped in light as with a
garment.
You stretch out the heavens
like a tent,
you set the beams of your
chambers on the waters,
you make the clouds your
chariot,
you ride on the wings of
the wind,
you make the winds your
messengers,
fire and flame your
ministers.

You set the earth on its
foundations,
so that it shall never be
shaken.
You cover it with the deep as
with a garment;
the waters stood above the
mountains.
At your rebuke they flee;
at the sound of your thunder they take to flight.
They rose up to the moun-
tains, ran down to the valleys
to the place that you ap-
pointed for them.
You set a boundary that they
may not pass,

so that they might not
again cover the earth.
You make springs gush forth
in the valleys;
they flow between the hills,
giving drink to every wild
animal;
the wild asses quench their
thirst.
By the streams the birds of
the air have their habitation;
they sing among the
branches.
From your lofty abode you
water the mountains;
the earth is satisfied with
the fruit of your work.

You cause the grass to grow
for the cattle,
and plants for people to use,
to bring forth food from the
earth,
and wine to gladden the
human heart,
oil to make the face shine,
and bread to strengthen the
human heart.
The trees of the LORD are wa-
tered abundantly,
the cedars of Lebanon that
he planted.
In them the birds build their
nests;
the stork has its home in
the fir trees.
The high mountains are for
the wild goats;

the rocks are a refuge for
the coneys.
You have made the moon to
mark the seasons;
the sun knows its time for
setting.
You make darkness, and it is
night,
when all the animals of the
forest come creeping out.
The young lions roar for their
prey,
seeking their food from
God.
When the sun rises, they
withdraw
and lie down in their dens.
People go out to their work
and to their labor until the
evening.

O Lord, how manifold are
your works!
In wisdom you have made
them all;
the earth is full of your
creatures.
Yonder is the sea, great and
wide,
creeping things innumerable
are there,
living things both small
and great.
There go the ships,
and Leviathan that you
formed to sport in it.

These all look to you

to give them their food in
due season;
when you give to them,
they gather it up;
when you open your hand,
they are filled with good
things.
When you hide your face,
they are dismayed;
when you take away their
breath, they die
and return to their dust.
When you send forth your
spirit, they are created;
and you renew the face of
the ground.

May the glory of the Lord
endure forever;
may the Lord rejoice in his
works—
who looks on the earth and it
trembles,
who touches the mountains
and they smoke.
I will sing to the Lord as long
as I live;
I will sing praise to my
God while I have being.
May my meditation be pleas-
ing to him,
for I rejoice in the Lord.
Let sinners be consumed from
the earth,
and let the wicked be no
more.
Bless the Lord, O my soul.
Praise the Lord!

Psalm 104

TABLEAU 9

Birds

Trübenbachtal on the way to Kirn

Liber Physica 6

Griffin – Ostrich – Peacock – Crane – Swan – Heron – Vulture –
Eagle – Stork – Goose – Duck – Cock and Hen – Capercaillie –
Partridge – Grouse – Falcon – Hawk – Sparrow Hawk –
Milan – Weho – Raven – Crows and Jackdaws – Carrion Crow –
Buzzard – Seagull – Dove – Turtledove – Parrot – Magpie –
Jay – Owl – Great Horned Owl – Little Owl – Cuckoo – Snipe –
Woodpecker – Sparrow – Titmouse – Blackbird – Thrush –
Lark – Kingfisher – Hoopoe – Quail – Nightingale – Starling –
Chaffinch – Goldfinch – Bunting – Warbler – White Wagtail –
Yellow Wagtail – Swallow – Golden Crested King – Bat –
Widderwalo – Honeybee – Housefly – Tree Cricket –
Grasshopper – Gnat – Bumblebee – Wasp – Glowworm –
Hornet – Grain Weevil – Silkworm – Beetle – and others

Many birds named by Hildegard in the sixth book of
Physica still live in this area. Yet, she describes seventy-five not
only native but also exotic birds. Also, according to medieval
classification, she adds insects as well as the bat here. Based
on what she knew, birds were created together with fish on
the fifth day of creation (Gen 1:20-23), and it seems important
to her to associate birds allegorically with human thought and
with the life of the soul. Thus, she identifies herself with an
eagle who shall lift itself from its indecisiveness just as John
the Evangelist. Hildegard describes the healing effects of these
birds, yet her recipes that call for the consumption of songbirds
provide an insight into medieval cooking habits that appear
to be quite problematic today.

"Since birds are lifted by their feathers into the air, and since they dwell everywhere in the air, they were thus created and positioned in order that the soul, with them, might feel and know the things which should be known."

The ostrich (strusz) is very hot and has the nature of beasts. It has the feathers of birds, but does not fly with them, since it runs quickly, just as a beast. It dwells on land, eating on pasture land.

The crane (grus) is hot and has a clean nature. It can both fly and move about on land. It flies willingly with a multitude and can very easily avoid snares. It has great strength in its neck, is straightforward and cautious, and has an alert disposition, a skill which forewarns it so no bird or beast can easily harm him.

The eagle (aquila) is very hot, just as if it were fiery. Having eyes more fiery than watery, it can boldly look into the sun. . . . Its flesh would be deadly for a person to eat. . . . Since it is suffused by the heat of the sun, and since it boldly looks at it, it is grim and has great sensibility in its heart.

The goose (anser) is hot and, also, from the air in which beasts live. . . . It cannot fly high. . . . It eats clean and unclean food. Because of its double nature, its flesh is weak and not good to eat. . . . People who are healthy are able to somehow survive when they have eaten its flesh.

The titmouse (meysa) is hot and dry. It is tame, flies in clear air, has healthy flesh, and is good for both sick and well people to eat.

TABLEAU 10

Beer

Kirn

Cerevisiam bibat!

"Drink beer!" Hildegard wrote this in her medical book *Causae et Curae*. Brewed in monasteries from 650 AD onwards, beer was made from oats and, occasionally, mingled with honey. And, even though beer in the Middle Ages contained far less alcohol than our beer today, Hildegard advised a modest consumption during the meals. She assumed that an excessive consumption of beer would lead to the dilution of the body's good juices. She also thought that people should drink beer and wine in winter and forgo water because at that time waters are not healthy due to the earth's humidity. In summer, she instead recommended drinking lukewarm water, for, because of the aridity of the earth, it would be less damaging than in winter. Yet, physically weak people should drink beer or wine mingled with water in summer.

"Beer makes the human flesh fat and gives a beautiful color to human faces by the power of the good juice of the cereal."

Hildegard especially recommended that melancholic people drink beer in order to raise their morale and support the regeneration of the soul's powers. Hildegard recognized already the preservative effect of hops as a plant, which she highly appreciated. Hops were cultivated in Germany since the eighth century and were later consistently added to the beer that was now mainly made from barley. In this region, beer is still brewed in the Kirn private brewery from hops, barley and water.

Heike Klaft

POEM

Hildegard's Visions

Open to the flow
 Open to the divine
  Open to the angels
   Open to the white light
 Open to God
   Hildegard receives her visions
 From the living light
Which becomes
 An exceedingly big and sparkling light
Hildegard writes
 Her visions onto wax tablets
Monk Volmar
 Watches and listens
  With curiosity
 He then transfers
 Hildegard's writings
Onto parchment or paper
Feel the presence of God
 Feel the flow of the divine
  Feel the wholeness
 We are life
 We are divine
We are the children of God

Karen S. E. Stock

Hildegard's Visionary Images

by Annette Esser

"But the visions I saw I did not perceive in dreams, or sleep, or delirium, or by the eyes of the body, or by the ears of the outer self, or in hidden places; but I received them while awake and seeing with a pure mind and the eyes and the ears of the inner self, in open places, as God willed it."

Hildegard of Bingen, *Declaration, Liber Scivias*

According to her own testimony, Hildegard had visions since her early childhood, yet, only in the forty-third year of her life (1141) did she begin to write them down. From this developed her first mystical work, *Scivias*. The title is an abbreviation for *Scito vias Domini* or *Scito vias lucis*—"Know the ways of the Lord" or "Know the ways of the Living Light." Hildegard believed that it was her divine mission to write down her visions in order for others to walk on this path of God, the Living Light. This is also what we do, when we follow the 27 meditation tableaux on the Hildegard Way with the 27 visions of *Scivias*—and this in the exact order given by Hildegard herself.

Hildegard experienced visions as a gift from God that she understood to be a grace. That does not mean that she was simply unprepared to receive them. As the female figure of *paupertas*—the poor in spirit—suggests, Hildegard herself sees an attitude of humility and mystical openness as a preparation for the divine vision.

Thus, several stages of visionary experience can be described:

1. Preparation in prayer and in existential dealing with philosophical questions such as humankind in the cos-

mos, the beginning and the end of the world, the origin and effect of evil after God's incarnation and human redemption.

2. The gift of mystical insight as a raw experience, which can be an experience of seeing (*visio*) or hearing (*auditio*) or also a purely intellectual insight.

3. Incorporated interpretation in initial notes, for example on wax tablets.

4. Reflexive interpretation and analyses over a longer period of time; here the work of others regarding interpretation and illumination is also important, for example writers and artists in the scriptorium.[3]

Although it was doubted in the nineteenth century whether Hildegard had in fact written all of the works that appeared under her name, the sisters of the new twentieth-century St. Hildegard's Abbey in Eibingen were the first to be able to prove her authorship.[4] Today, it is assumed that she herself put hand to the edition of her oeuvre in the Rupertsberg scriptorium. At any rate, in her mystical works, *Scivias* and the *Liber Divinorum Operum*, we find a clear order of her visions. This order follows a system that in the sense of the early scholastic theology of her time, the twelfth century, can be named a *summa theologiae*, a systematic visionary theology. This is also displayed in the order of her visions in three books (in the *Liber Scivias*) which expresses her understanding of creation:

"Book One: The Creator and Creation"—the first time of the history of salvation;

"Book Two: The Redeemer and Redemption"—the time with and since the incarnation of the Son of God;

"Book Three: The History of Salvation Symbolized by a Building"—the time of the church.

The historic time in which Hildegard worked on her first mystical work can be dated quite precisely. She began it at her time on the Disibodenberg (1112–1115); at the Synod of Trier (1147–1148), where Pope Eugene III personally commended that she continue writing; and she completed it in her time in the newly founded women's monastery on the Rupertsberg:

> *"These visions took place and these words were written in the days of Henry, Archbishop of Mainz, and of Conrad, King of the Romans, and of Cuno, Abbot of Disibodenberg, under Pope Eugene."*
> (Hildegard of Bingen, *Declaration, Liber Scivias*)

In Hildegard's lifetime eight more manuscripts were created; two more were copied after her death (1179) before the introduction of book printing in the fifteenth century. Two manuscripts remained in her convent, the so-called *Riesenkodex* that includes (nearly) all of Hildegard's writings, and the *Rupertsberg Scivias Codex* with its unique original miniatures that we now can admire on the whole Hildegard Way.

Regarding the question of whether Hildegard herself was also the artist of these famous illuminations, we first need to realize that in medieval thinking the real "artist" is the one who has the vision and is not the mere holder of the pencil or brush (just as one might say the composer is more important than the mere performer). However, in the technical sense, today's research largely agrees that Hildegard herself was not the "artist." Yet, after art-historical research had assumed for a long time that, because of the necessary, complex process of calligraphy and illumination, the miniatures were probably created by monks in a professional scriptorium, such as in Trier or Andernach, newer research increasingly assumes that the *Rupertsberg Scivias Codex* was in fact created during her lifetime and under her supervision (and maybe hand) in the Rupertsberg scriptorium. Recently Sr. Maura Zátonyi discovered the "hand" of Hildegard in the third handwritten correction that can be recognized on the old black and white photographs of the medieval original of the Rupertsberg *Scivias* (today in the Maria Laach Abbey); and she regards as accepted the view "that Hildegard herself has personally co-operated in working on the codex and the illuminations" and that she "herself has possibly influenced the illuminations and inspired them with her own ideas."[5]

Interestingly, there is also an argument that raises the question of the quality of the miniatures. The supporters of the assumption of codex production outside of Hildegard's scriptorium were the first to admit that even if we know about nuns writing (*scribens libris*), "we have only little knowledge about nuns illuminating."[6] Today it is just the observation of the imperfection and incomplete state of some of the miniatures that allows us to assume that the grand Rupertsberg codex was not made in a professional scriptorium. Albert Derolez explains this by saying that the codex originates from the work of devoted yet "poorly instructed and in essence unlearned female illuminators"; herewith he sees this as a further confirmation that the Rupertsberg nuns not only produced the text but also the miniatures in their own workshop."[7]

At any rate, the manuscript of *Scivias* that today we regard as the "original one" and from which all photographs are taken—including all those on the Hildegard Way—is a calligraphic and artistic work of the Eibingen nuns; however, this work was carried out between 1927 and 1933. This is because the medieval original was lost in the bombing of Dresden during World War II, where of all places it had been brought from the Wiesbaden *Landesarchiv* for safekeeping. So, it is merely thanks to fortunate circumstances or wise foresight that today we have the substitute original of *Scivias*. Thus the chronicle of Saint Hildegard Abbey, founded in 1904, tells us that the sisters planned at first to produce a copy of all the miniatures for their abbess and their abbey because the medieval original by then—after the time of secularization and therewith after the closing of the Eibingen monastery at the beginning of the nineteenth century—was in the Wiesbaden museum (*Landesarchiv*); yet the sisters wished to look at the illuminations in their original colors and not merely in the black and white photographs that only were possible at that time. Over the course of time the decision was made that the whole codex including the text should be copied. Thus, under the artistic guidance of calligrapher Anna Simons of Bonn, three sisters undertook a ten-year process of creating a copy of the medieval twelfth-century original. The basis of their work was not only the black and white photos but also a close examination of the medieval original that could be borrowed from Wiesbaden and brought to the abbey for ten months. Sr. Adelgundis reported the technically challenging work process:

> The miniatures and the text of the photographs were at first traced; then the tracings were transferred onto parchment. Only then did the writing and painting begin. With constant checking of the original manuscript or the photographs, the second manuscript of the *Scivias* was formed in this way in painstaking detailed work. Fine brushes were used for the miniatures as well as the initials. The application of gold and silver leaf required much preparatory work in order to align it best with the technique of the old codex.

For all the laborious, diligent and ever new, creative, and imaginative work of her sisters and also the monks who worked on this over the centuries, we can only be thankful today. For us, the visionary images and the illuminations are an awesome achievement.

All pilgrims on the Hildegard Way are now invited to look at, as well as to meditate and deeply reflect on, all the twenty-seven visionary images of *Scivias*.

STAGE 3

Kirn –
St. Johannisberg /
Skywalk –
Brunkenstein Ruin–
Dhaun Castle –
Simmertal –
Weiler –
Monzingen

3

Kirn – St. Johannisberg / Skywalk – Brunkenstein Ruin– Dhaun Castle – Simmertal – Weiler – Monzingen

Length 18.2 km – ca. 5.5 hrs. – Ascent 485 m – Descent 497 m

Kirn is located in the Protestant Western part of the Naheland. Appropriately, the third information tableau is about Hildegard as an early Protestant (**Tableau 11**).

The path from Kirn leads to the heights of St. Johannisberg and the Skywalk; from there, we have a wonderful view of the Nahe Valley and an old mining site. "The Meditation Tableau" at the St. Johannisberg Protestant Church invites to reflect about the soul and body of the human being and

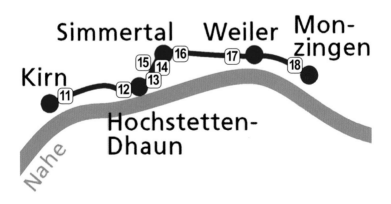

Along the Hildegard Way (above);
St. Johannisberg Church (right)

his/her life-journey (**Tableau 12**). The panoramic view at the Skywalk provides the opportunity to reflect upon Hildegard's book on metals (**Tableau 13**). There is also an opportunity to eat on the terrace of the Landhaus restaurant.

From the peak, the path leads deeper and deeper into the forest. In the midst of it, there is the Brunkenstein ruin. The topic of the information tableau there is Hildegard's book on reptiles—toads, serpents, dragons and other primeval and legendary creatures (**Tableau 14**).

From the forest, a side-path leads to Dhaun Castle. There, we are invited to consider more intensely Hildegard's music, which can be also be heard at all the meditation tableaux (**Tableau 15**). Below, at the old town hall in Simmertal, we find an information tableau about Hildegard's correspondence (**Tableau 16**). The Hildegard Way from Simmertal then leads to the old vineyard village of Weiler. In front of an old vineyard press we find a tableau about the history of viticulture and Hildegard's teachings regarding grapevines (**Tableau 17**). The stage of this day ends in Monzingen.

Dhaun Castle

TABLEAU 11

Hildegard as an Early "Protestant"

In the Protestant St. Johannisberg Church

"Saint Hildegard's prophecy about the papists and the named clergy, whose fulfillment has begun and shall be completed in our times." A Prologue by Andreas Osiander 1527.

Hildegard of Bingen (1098–1179) lived long before the Reformation, when the Christian church of the Holy Roman Empire was not yet split into "Catholic" and "Protestant" churches. A glance at church history justifies not merely calling her a "Catholic saint" but also identifying her as a "representative of the pre-Reformation" in Germany, whose critiques of the church were invoked by the reformers.

Thus, Andreas Osiander (1498–1552), a staunch follower of Luther's theology, who as the first Protestant minister in Nuremberg enforced the Reformation there, published two writings containing prophecies in 1527. Included in these was the text quoted above, which, as he said, he had found in Nuremberg's Carthusian Monastery.

This text contains Hildegard's exhortation to the clergy threatened by decay; it served as proof that Hildegard in the role of prophetess had already foretold the decline of the papal church in the twelfth century. Luther himself apparently never concerned himself with Hildegard, but one of his most resolute followers, Flacius Illyricus (1520–1575), stylized Hildegard as a kind of prototype for a precursor of Martin Luther and even identified her even as "Lutheran."

By drawing on Hildegard's ideas that were critical of the church, the Reformation was able to use her recognizable name to promote its interests. Therefore, Hildegard can indeed be called an early "Protestant."

Eveline Waterboer

TABLEAU 12

Soul and Body

St. Johannisberg Church

Liber Scivias I.4

PILGRIM'S REFLECTION

What do body, spirit and soul mean to me?

_____

_____

_____

_____

_____

_____

_____

_____

_____

_____

_____

_____

_____

_____

_____

_____

"Then I saw a most great and serene splendor, flaming, as it were, with many eyes, with four corners pointing to the four parts of the world, which was manifest to me in the greatest mystery to show me the secret of the Supernal Creator; and in it appeared another splendor like the dawn, containing in itself a brightness of purple lightning. And behold! I saw on the earth people carrying milk in earthen vessels and making cheeses from it; and one part was thick, and from it strong cheeses were made; and one part was thin, and from it weak cheeses were curdled; and one part was mixed with corruption; and from it bitter cheeses were formed. And I saw the image of a woman who had a perfect human form in her womb. And behold! By the secret design of the Supernal Creator that form moved with vital motion, so that a fiery globe that had no human lineaments possessed the heart of that form and touched its brain and spread itself through all its members."

In this fourth vision of the first book of *Scivias*, we see on the left the making of the human being, body and soul, and the inseparable connection to the Creator symbolized by the ray of light. The journey of the soul in the course of life is depicted on the right side: as it is inundated by the waters, torn apart by wild beasts, squeezed in the wine press, and chained by the evil one.

O Lᴏʀᴅ, you have searched me and known me. . . .
You hem me in, behind and before,
>and lay your hand upon me. . . .
Where can I go from your spirit?
>Or where can I flee from your presence?
If I ascend to heaven, you are there;
>if I make my bed in Sheol, you are there.
If I take the wings of the morning
>and settle at the farthest limits of the sea,
even there your hand shall lead me,
>and your right hand shall hold me fast.
If I say, "Surely the darkness shall cover me,
>and the light around me become night,"
even the darkness is not dark to you;
>the night is as bright as the day,
>for darkness is as light to you.

For it was you who formed my inward parts;
>you knit me together in my mother's womb.
I praise you, for I am fearfully and wonderfully made.
>Wonderful are your works;
that I know very well.
>My frame was not hidden from you,
when I was being made in secret,
>intricately woven in the depths of the earth.
Your eyes beheld my unformed substance.
In your book were written
>all the days that were formed for me,
>when none of them as yet existed.
How weighty to me are your thoughts, O God!
>How vast is the sum of them!
I try to count them—they are more than the sand;
>I come to the end —I am still with you.

O that you would kill the wicked, O God,
>and that the bloodthirsty would depart from me—
those who speak of you maliciously,
>and lift themselves up against you for evil!
Do I not hate those who hate you, O Lᴏʀᴅ?
>And do I not loathe those who rise up against you?
I hate them with perfect hatred;
>I count them my enemies.
Search me, O God, and know my heart;
>test me and know my thoughts.
See if there is any wicked way in me,
>and lead me in the way everlasting.

Psalm 139:1, 5, 7-24

Liber Divinorum Operum I.1

TABLEAU 13

Metals

St. Johannisberg Skywalk

Liber Physica 9

Gold – Silver – Lead – Tin – Copper –
Brass – Iron – Steel – Mercury

The Skywalk opens up a view of the Nahe Valley and the old stone quarry. In this region, there has been mining since Celtic and Roman times. In medieval times, the high need for metals (for armaments, swords and tools) led to increased ore mining throughout the Holy Roman Empire. In the ninth, last, and also shortest book of her *Liber Physica*, Hildegard lists nine metals in hierarchical order. Thereby, she envisions the formation of metals at the beginning of creation. She assigns attributes to the metals that range from practical use to religious meaning; along the same lines, these are also described in her visions.

"In the beginning, the spirit of the Lord was carried over the waters and the waters overflowed the earth. . . . And where the fiery power that flows in water penetrated the earth, the fire of the water transformed the earth into **gold***.*

Where the purity of the flooding water penetrated the earth, that purity transformed itself and the earth with it suffused into **silver.** *Where the fluctuation of the water penetrated the earth, moved by the wind, it and the earth transfused were changed into steel and iron. . . .*

Iron *is naturally very hot and therefore is strong. Its strength is useful for many things. . . .*

Steel *is very hot and is the very strongest form of iron. It nearly represents the divinity of God, whence the devil flees and avoids it."*

Hildegard of Bingen

TABLEAU 14

Reptiles

Brunkenstein Ruin

Liber Physica 6

Dragon – Poisonous Serpent – Slowworm – Toad – Frog –
Tree Frog – Salamander – Newt – Lizard – Spider – Viper –
Basilisk – Scorpion – Tarantula – Tyriaca – Scherzbedra –
Earthworm – Snail

In the ruins of Brunkenstein castle, we may think less about science and more about stories such as the fairy tale of *Frog Prince*, or the saga of *Siegfried* and his bath in dragon's blood in the middle of the forest, or on the powerful effect of the basilisk's tooth in *Harry Potter and the Chamber of Secrets*. In the eighth book of *Physica*, Hildegard lists eighteen dangerous and poisonous reptiles that do not all exist, at least according to our knowledge today. In her time, when the longing for stories was particularly strong, mythical creatures were fascinating, and a certain serpent embodying the devil in the story of Paradise was especially frightening (cf. Gen 3:1). Also, even though medieval people had never seen some of these creatures, they believed in their existence because they could admire their relics. Thus, when Hildegard gives us a recipe for the use of "dragon's blood," she was convinced that the resin (!) bearing that name was literally that.

"One whose eyes get dark shall also put a little dragon's blood into water for a short while, take this blood out of water and brush carefully his eyelids and eyelashes with this blood."

Hildegard of Bingen

TABLEAU 15

Hildegard's Music

In Dhaun Castle

Detail from *Liber Divinorum Operum* III.2

"Then I also composed and sang chant with melody to the praise of God and the Saints, without being taught by anyone, since I had never studied neumes or any chant at all."

Hildegard of Bingen, *Vita* II.2

Until a few decades ago, Hildegard's music was practically unknown. In the last thirty years, scholars and musicians have published and interpreted her work with increasing interest. Hildegard's musical and poetic compositions amount to 159 songs, seventy-seven of which belong to the *Symphonia harmoniae caelestium revelationum* and the rest to the morality play *Ordo virtutum*. This is the most music of any composer to have survived prior to the twelfth century.

According to the testimony of Hildegard herself, her visions included not only images but also voices, words, and music. Her experience of the ineffable, processed by her sensitivity, her unconditional love of nature, and her commitment to teaching, all turn into original compositions of great spiritual and expressive strength. Her poetic texts, written in a particularly idiosyncratic Latin that no writer would dare to correct, are highly suggestive and expressive.

Her melodies are unique and do not conform to the usual patterns of Gregorian modes. Many of Hildegard's songs have a great melodic range that makes us think that, together with the nuns of her community, she sang with great vocal freedom and mastery. Listening to the music of Hildegard allows us to get a little closer to transcendence.

Margarida Barbal Rodoreda

TABLEAU 16

Hildegard's Correspondence

Simmertal Town Hall

Detail from *Liber Divinorum Operum* III.5

*"O king, it is imperative for you to have foresight in all your affairs.
For in a mystic vision I see you like a little boy or a madman living
before Living Eyes. . . . Beware therefore that the almighty king
does not lay you low."*

From no other woman in history prior to the sixteenth
century (Teresa of Ávila) is such an extensive correspondence
preserved as that of Hildegard of Bingen. The famous abbess

herself probably took care of editing her correspondence of over thirty years in order that it should be kept for posterity. This was because letters were the most important medium of her time and letters by famous personalities were read aloud publicly like sermons.

From the 390 extant letters, we know that Hildegard corresponded with all social classes, including popes, bishops, abbots and abbesses, prelates, priests, monks and nuns as well as simple lay people, especially women. Everybody asked for her advice on medical issues, human catastrophes, or questions of faith.

Whereas in her first preserved letter to Bernard of Clairvaux, she calls herself a "poor little female," in later letters she speaks powerfully in the name of the "living light."

Thus, it was possible for her to sharply denounce the situation in the church and society of her time; she even dared to accuse Emperor Frederick Barbarossa, who had provided her Rupertsberg monastery with a charter of protection, of "blindness." This shows that not only herself but also her contemporaries believed that God spoke through her. People wanted to hear her words, the words of the *trumpet of God*.

TABLEAU 17

Wine

Old Wine Press near Weiler

"A grapevine (vitis) has fiery heat and moisture in it. The fire is so strong as to change its sap to a flavor that other trees and herbs do not have."

Hildegard of Bingen, *Liber Physica* III.54

Since Roman times and until today, grapevines have been cultivated along the banks of the Rhine and the Moselle, and in the Palatinate. Roman agricultural skills were already highly developed. After the collapse of the Roman Empire, this culture was lost. It was only in the Frankish period under Charlemagne (747–814), who enacted wine laws (*Capitulare de villis*), that wine culture underwent a renaissance. The vineyards were owned by the nobility, the church and monasteries. By Hildegard's time in the twelfth century, viticulture had become widespread.

Hildegard studied old and new applications of medical wines and tinctures from wine and published them in her writings and during her journeys. Thus, she knew that wine makes water drinkable without causing illness, is excellent to preserve food, and is especially effective as a solvent in order to produce plant extracts from healing herbs.

According to her, grapevines offered even more useful products such as: water from the vine trunk, ashes, juice pressed from the green parts of the plant, grape-kernels, and wine-yeast. All of these could be useful for healing purposes. Also, thickening grape juice made an exquisite product to sweeten drinks and food. Hildegard's move to Bingen on the Rhine brought her into the center of the vine growing and trade of her time.

Wilhelm Schweinhardt

SONG

O nobilissima viriditas

O nobilissima viriditas
O most noble greenness,

quae radicas in sole
you are rooted in the sun,

et quae in candida serenitate luces in rota
and in bright serenity you shine in a wheel

quam nulla terrena excellentia comprehendit,
that no earthly excellence comprehends,

tu circumdata es amplexibus divinorum mysteriorum
you are surrounded by embraces of divine mysteries

Tu rubes ut aurora
You redden like the dawn

et ardes ut solis flamma
and you burn like the flame of the sun.

Hildegard of Bingen[1]

Viriditas—Green Power of Life

by Annette Esser

In her song, *O nobilissima viriditas*, Hildegard sings about the noble power of viridity: it is green like the plants of the earth, but also golden like the sun and red like the dawn. That means *viriditas* is not just about nature—it is a power that is connected to the divine mystery.

As a friend of Hildegard, I imagine her walking through the cloister, considering and playing with certain words. These are words that do not resonate in the German language, yet are connected only in Latin (and quite a bit also in English!): *viriditas* (green power of life), *vir* (male power), *virtus* (virtue), *virga* (branch), *virgo* (virgin) and *virginitas* (virginity).

Thus, Hildegard connects the virgin and the branch, associates virginity with viridity and looks at virtue as a male power that paradoxically is inherent to virgins because men have become effeminate.

Hildegard loved the thought that a virgin "stands in the unsullied purity of paradise." To portray this, I have made a sculpture from clay. It is based on a description in a letter from Mistress Tengswich of Andernach to Hildegard of Bingen:

> *"We have, however also heard about certain strange and irregular practices that you countenance. They say that on feast days your virgins stand in the church with unbound hair when singing the psalms and that as part of their dress they wear white, silk veils, so long that they touch the floor. Moreover, it is said that they wear crowns of gold filigree, into which are inserted crosses on both sides and the back, with a figure of the Lamb on the front, and that they adorn their fingers with golden rings."*[2]

Today, what shall we do with Hildegard's thoughts and songs about *viriditas*?

As a theologian, I see Hildegard not merely as a woman mystic but also as a naturalist and medical practitioner who investigates the powers of nature and describes their healing effects on human beings. Therefore, I say: *viriditas* is the green power of life. The green power of life is divine power. Divine power is the power of creation and it is healing power.

Yet, there is a question about whether or not Hildegard's language can be taken seriously by modern science and medicine. For, we can observe a rift in the assessment of *Physica*, that is, her natural history, for example by healing practitioners as compared to university-trained medical doctors.

Here, I remember a dialogue that I had with my own sister, who is a professor of immunology at Düsseldorf University. As we talked about how "biology" really means "knowledge about life," she simply said that, of course, this science could only describe life processes. Yet, what life is itself, and even why there is life at all and not just absence of life, this is a philosophical question that modern science neither can nor would like to answer.

Now, this reminded me of a story by Danish philosopher Sören Kierkegaard: A person enters a shop that has signs in its windows on which is written, "We take care of your laundry!" As he asks about whether his laundry could be done here, he gets the answer: "Of course, we do not wash your laundry here. We just sell the signs that say, 'We wash your laundry.'"

Very different from these signs, Hildegard's talk about *viriditas* is not just about signs saying "Life is green power" (this would in any case merely be a tautology). Hildegard also did not merely describe natural processes from the objective perspective of a researcher that we could probably better study in scientific books today. No, I think that when Hildegard talks and sings about *viriditas*, then she speaks not only about God as origin of all life, but also about how, in all life on this

earth and in us human beings, divine power is at work. That means that not only does she describe processes of growing in nature, but she also interprets the processes that she observes as divine power and thus a name of God him/herself. God for her is *caritas* (divine love), *sapientia* (wisdom), and also *viriditas* (green power of life).

The 2016 International Hildegard Conference in Bingen was about "*Viriditas*–Grünkraft–Green Power of Life." In our time of climate change, growing environmental destruction and species extinction in the world of flora and fauna, we too are concerned with the question and the challenge of sustainable development on our mother planet, Earth.

The point is the need for us humans to understand that if we continue to exploit nature with a rather distant attitude; if we do not understand that we are sawing off the branch on which we sit, so to speak; if we do not realize that, as a part of life, we are called to ethically take responsibility for sustainable development, then we will erase life itself on our planet.

Yet, when we realize that if we truly understand that, because of our position as humans in the center of the cosmos, the further development of life on our planet depends on us, then, in a synergy, in a co-operation between God and humans, earth and nature can go on to develop in a life-affirming, positive, constructive and sustainable way of life. In Hildegard's language it is as if humans would let flourish their virginal as well as their male virtue. Or it is as if the salespersons in the shop reflected about what really was written on their signs: *viriditas*—this is not just a word, but a power with which we humans can and must work together in synergy.

Annette Esser, *Virgin Hildegard*, clay-work, 40 cm, 2013

STAGE 4

Monzingen –
Nussbaum –
Bad Sobernheim –
Staudernheim –
Disibodenberg

4

Monzingen – Nussbaum – Bad Sobernheim – Staudernheim – Disibodenberg

Length 13.2 km – ca. 3.5 hrs. – Ascent 112 m – Descent 132 m

Today's fourth stage guides us from the 1,200-year-old vineyard village of Monzingen into the center of the Hildegard Way.

Thus, the Disibodenberg, where Hildegard lived for nearly 40 years of her life (from 1112 through 1150), is right in the middle of the hiking route and is the heart of the "land of Hildegard." Also, the central topic of this stage is Hildegard's art of healing, and this is the main reason why many people concern themselves with the saint today.

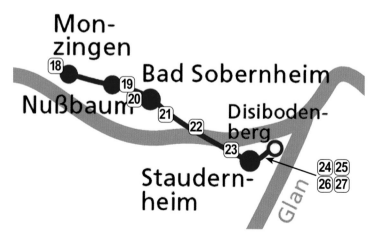

Herbal garden in Monzingen (above, left); horse at the outskirts of Nussbaum (above, right)

The morning starts at the herbal garden near Monzingen Protestant Church. There we find the information on Hildegard's book on plants (**Tableau 18**), in addition to the culinary herbs that grow here.

Through meadows and vineyards, the pilgrimage path guides us to the nearby village of Nussbaum. The topic of the next information tableau near the paddocks outside of Nussbaum is Hildegard's book on animals (**Tableau 20**).

The path leads us further to Bad Sobernheim, which is renowned as a spa and especially for its healing-mud cures, according to Pastor Felke. Also, after World War II, this spa-town, with its Jewish children's home, became known as an important recreation area for Jews in Germany and beyond.

The next meditation tableau, "*Synagoga*," whose theme is almost accidental in Hildegard's systematic order, fits this location well (**Tableau 21**). Yet, the tableau is deliberately not installed in front of the old Jewish synagogue (*Kulturhaus*) but in front of the Malteser chapel, with a view of the synagogue and its Star of David, in order to symbolize that Hildegard's

Old town and marketplace of Bad Sobernheim

Tympanon with crucification group at the historic Disibodenberg Chapel in Bad Sobernheim

vision does not represent Jewish self-understanding but merely a Christian perspective of Judaism.

At the *Priorhof*, the herbal garden of the Bad Sobernheim local museum, the information tableau is about Hildegard's medical herbs (**Tableau 19**). This same tableau is still found in the little Hildegard Garden in Duchroth.

The pilgrim can now look forward to a visit to the Disibodenberg chapel, where one can admire the sculpture "Virgin Hildegard," whose image is on the front of every pilgrimage passport as well as the pilgrimage book. This late Gothic chapel, which at one time belonged to the Sobernheim farm of the Disibodenberg monastery, has been used for various purposes over the centuries; just very recently (2019), it was completely rebuilt as a brewery with a restaurant ("Denkmals"). And now the pilgrim may also try the new Hildegard brew—not beer— that is brewed from spelt, hops, elderberry, parsley and ginger.

The Hildegard Way then leads along the Barefoot Path where Hildegard's art of healing is the focus of her nature study in *Physica* (**Tableau 22**, *Causae et Curae*). After crossing the Nahe River, the pilgrim is encouraged to visit the natural

The Nahe River in Bad Sobernheim

Disibodenberg ruin site in winter

museum in Staudernheim, where the tableau dedicated to Hildegard's nature study stands (**Tableau 23**, *Physica*).

At the end of the day in Staudernheim, at the foot of the Disibodenberg, one can meditate on the tableau of Hildegard's vision of the angels at the Catholic church (**Tableau 24**) and on her vision of the Redeemer at the Protestant church (**Tableau 25**).

Since we are approaching the Disibodenberg, the text of the day is about Hildegard's entrance into the Disibodenberg monastery on All Saints Day, 1112.

Longing for St. Hildegard of Bingen and Christus Medicus

As an empty shell
We are
Longing for
The touch of the divine
Longing
For the kiss of spirit
Longing for
The life-force
That we once knew
As children
Longing for
Physical strength as we age
Longing for
Mental clarity for our confusion
Longing for
Relief of our fears, phobias
Anxieties, anger and rage
Longing for

The release of physical pain
In our bodies
Longing for
The curing of our illnesses
Longing for
Liberation of our earthly prisons
Longing for
The infusion of
The white light
That St. Hildegard of Bingen
Once received
Longing for
The Savior
Christus Medicus
Longing
For the healing
Of our soul, mind and body

Karen S. E. Stock

TABLEAU 18

Plants

Herbal Garden at Monzingen Protestant Church

"The six works of creation," section from *Liber Scivias* II.1

Hildegard's book on plants is the first and by far the most comprehensive book of *Physica*. She writes not only about the beneficial and harmful effects of 217 herbs, grains, vegetables and flowers, but also about animal products and other natural resources.

Regarding herbs, a distinction between culinary herbs, spices or healing herbs cannot easily be made; as teas, tinctures or ointments, they can have healing effects on certain ailments for some people, for example fennel, sage or calendula.

Besides many healing herbs (cf. **Tableau 19**), Hildegard names these important plants:

The best grain is **spelt**. *It is hot, rich, and powerful. It is milder than other grains.*

Galingale is totally hot . . . and is powerful. A person with a burning fever should drink pulverized galingale.

Feverfew is of moderate heat and somewhat dry. It is good for a healthy person. . . . It restores strength to an ill person whose body is almost completely failing.

Wild thyme is hot and balanced. . . . When the brain is ill, as if it is empty, he should pulverize the thyme and mix it with fine whole wheat flour in water. He should make little cakes and eat them often and his brain will be better.

The **nettle** is very hot in its own way. It is not at all good eaten raw, because of its harshness. But, when it newly sprouts from the ground, it is good when cooked, as food for humans. It purges his stomach and takes mucus away from it.

TABLEAU 19

Medical Herbs

Bad Sobernheim *Priorhof*

Liber Physica 1

Panic Grass – Psyllium – Lungwort – Hart's-Tongue Fern –
Yellow Gentian – Goatsbeard – Fenugreek – Sysemera –
Hemlock – Woundwort – Sanicle – Fern – Arum – Spurge –
Belladonna – Tithymal – Conquefoil – Mandrake –
Sunnewirbel – Lilim – Sage – Rue – Fennel – Prickly Lettuce –
Plantain – Southernwood – Wormwood – Henbane – Tansy –
Oregano – Yarrow – Dittany – German Chamomile –
Black Nightshade – Calendula – Mullein – Cornflower –
Columbine – Celandine – Ivy – Marsh mallow – Valerian –
Catnip – Herb Robert – Comfrey – Flax – Chickweed –
Goutweed – Vervain – Arnica – Bloodwort – Cranesbill –
Bennet – Madder – Masterwort – Asafoetida – Aloe – Balsam –
Meranda – Vetch – Primrose – Butterbur – Coltsfood

Hildegard's book on plants is the first and by far the most comprehensive book of *Physica*. She writes about the beneficial as well as harmful effects of 217 plants and other food products. Many herbs that may have already proved to be of value in Hildegard's medical work at the monastic hospice are still important in today's nutrition science and phyto-medicine. Thus, in case of fever, she recommends remedies with panic grass, fenugreek or masterwort; those who have a cold, cough or sore throat will find cranesbill or tansy helpful; fennel is good for the stomach and in case of digestion problems. Yellow gentian, dittany or mullein are good for the heart; bleeding can be stilled with sage; wounds shall be treated with yarrow and eczemas with celandine; women's menstrual pain can be stilled with German chamomile; and there are also remedies for ailments of the soul such as primrose, balsam or bennet; and, finally, Hildegard recommends mandrake and wormwood as universal remedies.

Masterwort (astrencia)—For any kind of fever, one should pound masterwort. Once it is shredded, he should pour half a glass of wine over it, and leave it overnight. In the morning, he should add wine to it, and drink it, before breakfast. If he does this for three to five days, he will be cured. This is because the heat of the masterwort tempered by heat and taken as a drink will drive out the fever, and when served at night, the wine will mix better.

Sage (selba) is of hot and dry nature, and grows more from the heat of the sun than from the moisture of the earth. It is useful against ill humors, since it is dry. It is good to eat, raw or cooked, for one whom noxious humors are troubling, since it checks them. Take sage and pulverize it. Eat this powder with bread and it will diminish the superfluidity of harmful humors in you.

Balsam (balsamon) is of royal nature. . . . If someone is insane, use the unguent to anoint his temples and neck. . . . This restores his right mind and good health.

Bennet (benedicta)—But, if someone is failing in all his corporeal powers, he should cook bennet in water, and often drink that water warm. He will recoup the powers of his body.

Mandrake (mandragora) is hot and a little bit watery. It grew from the same earth which formed Adam, and resembles the human a bit. . . . Whoever suffers some infirmity in the head should eat from the top of the plant, in whatever way he wishes. If he suffers in his neck, he should eat from its neck; if in the back, from its back. . . . In whatever part he is ailing, he should eat from the similar part of this image, and he will be better.

Wormwood (wermuda) or **Absinthe** is very hot and has much strength. It is the principal remedy for all ailments. Pour a sufficient amount of its juice into warm wine. For one who has headache, wet the entire head, from the eyes to the ears and the neck. Do this at night, upon going to bed. Cover the whole head with a woolen cap, until morning, and it will suppress the pain of the swollen head. It will chase away the pain that pulsates on the head from gicht, as well as the pain inside the head.

TABLEAU 20

Animals

Nussbaum

Liber Physica 7

Elephant – Camel – Lion – Cheetah – Leopard – Bear – Unicorn –
Tiger – Panther – Elk – Horse – Ass – Dromedary – Deer –
Roe Deer – Ibex – Bison – Ox – Sheep – Goat – Pig – Hare – Wolf –
Mule – Dog – Fox – Beaver – Otter – Monkey – Marmoset – Cat –
Lynx- Badger – Polecat – Hedgehog – Squirrel – Hamster –
Marten – Water Marten – Sable – Ermine – Wild Rabbit – Mole –
Weasel – Mouse – Rat – Shrew – Flea – Ant

According to the biblical creation story, both animals and
human beings were created on the sixth day and, therefore,
they are most closely related to each other. In the seventh
book of *Physica*, Hildegard writes first about exotic animals,
not domestic ones. These are important in the Bible, in myth
and in heraldry. Also, human beings have always identified
themselves with certain animals.

Hildegard writes: *"Animals, which run around on land and
live on the earth, represent the thoughts and meditations a person
brings to a completion in work."*

Lion (leo)—*The lion is very hot and has got some human power, yet
it possesses the nature of animals. If its bestial nature did not detain
him, he would be able to penetrate stones. The lion recognizes a human
being. If, in its fury, the lion injures a person, it grieves afterward.*

Horse (equus)—*The horse is more hot than cold and has a good nature. It has such great strength that it does not know it has it. It always
wants to go walk in front, eats clean things.*

Roe Deer (rech) *is of a moderate nature. It is gentle and has a clean nature. It gladly climbs mountains and seeks air that is not too hot and not too cold, but temperate. In the mountains it forages for herbs that grow from this sort of air. They are good, healthy foods. Its flesh is good for healthy and sick people.*

Cow and ox (bos)—*The ox is cold and dry in temperament. Where there is an ox, airy spirits do not make enmity for a human being, nor can they create their various illusions. The ox is clean and in ancient days was often given to God as a whole burnt offering. . . . In moderation, a healthy and a sick person, a hot one and a cold one, can eat and drink milk and butter and cheese from the milk of the cow.*

Dog (canis)—*The dog which is perfect is very hot and has a common and natural affinity with human ways. It senses and understands the human being, loves him, willingly dwells with him and is faithful.*

TABLEAU 21

The Synagogue

Bad Sobernheim

Liber Scivias I.5

PILGRIM'S REFLECTION

What do I know about the history of Judaism and synagogues in Germany?

What do Moses and the prophets mean to me?

_____

_____

_____

_____

_____

_____

_____

_____

_____

_____

_____

_____

_____

_____

_____

_____

"After this I saw the image of a woman."

In the fifth vision of the first book of *Scivias*, Hildegard envisions the *Synagogue* as a female figure. She symbolizes Judaism which Hildegard valued highly. In her heart stands Moses with the medieval Jew's hat upholding the tablets with the Ten Commandments; and, in her womb, all the prophets and prophetesses of the Old Testament are assembled.

The text on the tableau tells us that Hildegard appreciated Judaism very much. This is true insofar as

> she time and again stresses the impact of Abraham, Moses, and the other prophets and also places herself in their tradition;

> she appreciates the books of the Old Testament and quotes extensively from them, especially from the Wisdom books;

> she names *Synagoga* as the mother of the incarnation of the Son of God (*mater incarnationis*) and thereby gives her the highest title, because for Hildegard, incarnation is at the heart of the history of redemption;

> for Hildegard, Judaism has a fundamental meaning in the whole history of redemption, even though after the incarnation the time of *Ecclesia* begins.

We may also observe that, in comparison with later images from the thirteenth century—for instance at Strasbourg Cathedral, where *Synagoga* is depicted blindfolded, with hands, and without Moses and the prophets in her womb—Hildegard's vision of *Synagoga* is still *relatively* positive.

Yet, all this does not alter the fact that Hildegard shared in the common opinion that "the Jews killed Jesus." In the vision, this is depicted in the blood-red color of the feet and the interpretation: *"For at the end of her time she killed the Prophet of the Prophets and therefore slipped and fell down herself."* This manner of speaking is devastating because for centuries it was used to justify pogroms against Jews. Thus in 1096, two years before Hildegard was born, the pogroms of Ashkenazi Jews in Speyer and Worms took place. And one could argue that, in the final analysis, this argument led to the Holocaust of the twentieth century. Therefore, unfortunately, it is too short-sighted to say that Hildegard's vision can only be understood in the context of her time, the twelfth century.

Rather, it is necessary to look critically at the whole of Christianity and its image of Judaism, including Hildegard's vision of *Synagoga*.

And all Christians, especially in Germany, need to ask themselves which images they have of Judaism and what position they take regarding the history of anti-Semitism and the pogroms of the Jews. This is exactly what the pilgrim's reflection is about.

> Say to wisdom, "You are my sister,"
> and call insight your intimate friend.
>
> Proverbs 7:4

TABLEAU 22

Causae et Curae

The Bad Sobernheim Barefoot Path

Liber Divinorum Operum I.3

This first medical work of Hildegard, *Causae et Curae* (*The Origin and Treatment of Illnesses*), contains a comprehensive description of the human condition. It begins with an explanation of the creation of the cosmos and the elements, of which the human being also consists. Subsequently, their development and different constitutions are depicted as well. In the unity of body and soul, the soul vitalizes the body, and at the same time it is connected with the Creator.

Hildegard sees the origins of illnesses in unhealthy habits related to nourishment, sleep, life-rhythms that cause illnesses and emotions, as well as in the suppression of one's own calling. We recognize in this knowledge, which was compiled 850 years ago, insights about today's psychosomatic medicine and psycho-neuro-immunology. According to Saint Hildegard, the relationship to God the Creator contributes essentially to well-being and healing.

She gives detailed instructions for recipes for all kinds of complaints from head to feet; to these belong fasting and diverse treatments for the removal of toxins, so-called options for detoxification, that still prove of value today.

The description of many life processes is amazing. Hildegard of Bingen is the first to name the female organs and their far-reaching functions. A central notion is *viriditas*—the green power of life; it affects not only plants and the earth but also the human being. Hildegard stresses the value of joy as well as of *discretio*, the right degree in everything. She reminds us of our responsibility for creation, to which we are related. This is also very relevant today.

Michael Ptok

TABLEAU 23

Physica

Museum of Nature, Staudernheim

Physica is one of two works of Hildegard's art of natural healing that originally were one. Comprising nine books, it contains plants, elements, trees, stones, fish, birds, animals, reptiles and metals. In them, Hildegard perceived and described beneficial or pathogenic effects, or no inherent effects, for the healing of humans and animals.

In addition to the historical research on these texts, there is a growing interest in a responsible application of the more than two thousand recipes in the context of naturopathy. Hildegard's art of healing is part of monastic medicine and Traditional European Medicine (TEM). Recent findings in medical history show that the descriptions provided by Saint Hildegard transcend the common knowledge of her time and are to be regarded as unique and original. Even if the implementation appears to be incomprehensible or does not fit with our understanding, which has evolved over the time, for example due to the protection of species, many of her recipes can still be used successfully today.

In medical practice, the many positive experiences reported by patients are decisive here. The spectrum comprises prophylactic aspects as well as treatments for manifold illnesses. According to her own testimony, it was always important for Hildegard to look at human beings in their integrity, that is, in their entire network of relations, and to take this into account in their path towards healing.

Michael Ptok

Welcome to the Museum Nahe der Natur in Staudernheim

TABLEAU 24

The Choirs of the Angels

Staudernheim Catholic Church

Liber Scivias I.6

PILGRIM'S REFLECTION

What image of angels do I have?

Do I believe in angels and their work?

THE CHOIRS OF ANGELS

"Then I saw in the secret places in the heights of Heaven . . . armies of heavenly spirits."

The sixth and last vision of the first book of *Scivias* is perceived today as a mandala. According to an old tradition, it shows the nine choirs of the angels ordered in circles around a beaming white center that symbolizes God. On the outside are the angels who, as God's messengers, are close to humans (guardian angels and archangels). In the midst are the angels that are close to God and who enshroud their faces (cherubim and seraphim). And in between are the angels that relate and work between God and humans: the virtues, powers, princedoms, dominations and thrones.

The emptiness in the inner circle also relates the vision to the biblical demand that we shall not make for ourselves an idol of God (Exod 20:4). Behind the visages of the angels that veil the face of God, we cannot see God directly.

In all that has been said about the armies of heavenly spirits, maybe the most important reality has not yet been named. For Hildegard, her visions were at the same time auditions. She not only speaks about angels—she hears them singing and she composes her music "with them." She assumes that all those who sing this music join in with the choirs of angels, on earth as in heaven.

> The LORD has established his throne in the heavens,
>   and his kingdom rules over all.
> Bless the LORD, O you his angels,
>   you mighty ones who do his bidding,
>   obedient to his spoken word.
> Bless the LORD, all his hosts,
>   his ministers that do his will.
>
> Psalm 103:19-21

SONG

O vos Angeli

O vos Angeli	O angels
qui custodis populos,	that guard the peoples,
quorum forma fulget	whose form gleams
in facie vestra,	in your faces,
et o vos Archangeli,	and O archangels
qui suscipitis animas	that receive the souls of
iustorum,	the just;
et vos Virtutes,	and you virtues,
Potestates,	powers,
Principatus,	princedoms,
Dominationes	dominations
et Throni,	and thrones,
qui estis computati	who are reckoned
in quintum secretum numerum,	in the mystical number of five,
et o vos Cherubim	and O you cherubim
et Seraphim,	and seraphim,
sigillum secretorum Dei, sit	seal of the secret things of God:
laus vobis,	Praise to you,
qui loculum antiqui cordis	who behold in the fountain
in fonte aspicitis.	the little place of the ancient heart.
Videtis enim	For you see
interiorem vim Patris	the inmost strength of the Father,
quae de corde illius spirat	which breathes from his heart
quasi facies.	like a face.
sit laus vobis,	Praise be to you,
qui loculum antiqui cordis	who behold in the fountain
in fonte aspicitis.	the little place of the ancient heart.

Hildegard of Bingen[1]

TABLEAU 25

The Redeemer

Staudernheim Protestant Church

Liber Scivias II.1

PILGRIM'S REFLECTION

What is the "original sin" all about
in my own understanding?

What does Christ as "redeemer" mean to me?

"And I, a person not glowing with the strength of strong lions . . . but a tender and fragile rib imbued with a mystical breath, saw a blazing fire, incomprehensible, inextinguishable, wholly living and wholly Life, with a flame in it in the color of the sky. . . . Then the same flame was in that fire, and that burning extended itself to a little clod of mud . . . and warmed it so that is was made flesh and blood, and blew upon it until it rose up a living human. When this was done, the blazing fire . . . offered to the human a white flower. . . . Its scent came to the human's nostrils, but he did not taste it with his mouth or touch it with his hands, and thus he turned away and fell into the thickest darkness, out of which he could not pull himself. . . . And in the earth appeared a radiance like the dawn. . . . And I saw a serene Man coming forth from this radiant dawn, Who poured out His brightness into the darkness . . . and struck the darkness such a strong blow that the person who was lying in it was touched by Him, took on a shining appearance and walked out of it upright. And so the serene Man Who had come out of the dawn shone more brightly than human tongue can tell, and made His way into the greatest height of inestimable glory, where he radiated in the plentitude of wonderful fruitfulness and fragrance.*

In the first vision of the second book of *Scivias*, Hildegard depicts the events of the whole history of salvation in a single image. The top and bottom circle symbolize the trinitarian God, whose sapphire-blue in the middle hints from the beginning at the incarnation of God in Jesus Christ. The transparent circle in the middle shows the work of the six days of creation. At the top right, Adam, the first human being, sniffs at the "flower of obedience," yet does not pick it. The "fallen Adam," depicted by the red figure, represents all humankind; he is redeemed by Christ who rises as the Son of God from the Father and who will take the human being anew into his divine light.

Therefore, just as sin came into the world through one man, and death came through sin, and so death spread to all because all have sinned—sin was indeed in the world before the law, but sin is not reckoned when there is no law. Yet death exercised dominion from Adam to Moses, even over those whose sins were not like the transgression of Adam, who is a type of the one who was to come.

But the free gift is not like the trespass. For if the many died through the one man's trespass, much more surely have the grace of God and the free gift in the grace of the one man, Jesus Christ, abounded for the many. And the free gift is not like the effect of the one man's sin. For the judgment following one trespass brought condemnation, but the free gift following many trespasses brings justification. If, because of the one man's trespass, death exercised dominion through that one, much more surely will those who receive the abundance of grace and the free gift of righteousness exercise dominion in life through the one man, Jesus Christ.

Therefore just as one man's trespass led to condemnation for all, so one man's act of righteousness leads to justification and life for all. For just as by the one man's disobedience the many were made sinners, so by the one man's obedience the many will be made righteous. But law came in, with the result that the trespass multiplied; but where sin increased, grace abounded all the more, so that, just as sin exercised dominion in death, so grace might also exercise dominion through justification leading to eternal life through Jesus Christ our Lord.

Romans 5:12-21

Second Station
in Hildegard's Life:
Entrance to
St. Disibod Monastery

by Annette Esser

On the eve of All Saints in the year 1112, three virgins of noble blood gathered with their families at the foot of the Disibodenberg. They wished to be admitted to the flourishing monastery of St. Disibod as recluses. These were high-born countess Jutta of Sponheim (born 1092, then twenty years old), her relative Hildegard of Bingen (born 1098, then fourteen years old), and another young virgin, who (perhaps) was also called Jutta.

The hill of Disibodenberg was known from time immemorial as a holy mountain; it had already been a sacred site in Celtic and Roman times. In the early seventh century, the Irish-Scottish missionary St. Disibod built beehive cells on the hillside and thus founded a first monastery with some companions. The foundation flourished and declined over the course of time. Under the protection and with the encouragement of Archbishop Ruthard of Mainz, twelve Benedictine monks came here at the beginning of the twelfth century and made a new start in the derelict buildings. In 1108, the foundation stone of the big St. Nicholas Church was laid. In 1112, the new monastery was still for the most part a construction site, and it would remain so for many years. The final consecration occurred only in 1143.

With the three virgins under the guidance of countess Lady Jutta of Sponheim, the monastery could finally expand with a women's cloister; in it, Lady Jutta of Sponheim, whose family had erected that women's cell in 1108, could build up and lead a women's community as magistra. With this, the Disibodenberg, like the majority of Benedictine monasteries since the beginning of the twelfth century, could develop into a double monastery. The monks of the male cloister also looked forward to this. The idea that women could "embody" the life of a monk "in its highest perfection" (Abbot Theoger of St. Georgen), found religious communities (for example, Herluca in Hirsau), and even direct a double monastery (e.g. the monastery of Fontevraud, founded in 1101 by Robert of Abrissel and led since 1115 by Abbess Petronella) embodied the new spirit of the time.

Lady Jutta had struggled hard for this day. Fascinated by the new reform movements of the time that were striving to return to the original life in Christ, she had vowed to renounce marriage during a severe illness at the age of twelve in 1104. And although many "noble and wealthy landowners" sought to marry her, she took the veil from Bishop Ruthard of Mainz at the age of fourteen (1106) against the wishes of her relatives.[2] Yet she was unable to pursue her other desire, namely to go on a pilgrimage to the Holy Land, of which the First Crusade in 1096 had brought much news. Instead, her brother Count Meinhard of Sponheim succeeded in preventing her, with the support of Bishop Otto of Bamberg. The bishop convinced Jutta that she could pursue her wish to renounce the world better in a cloister, and he arranged for her entry into the newly founded monastery of Disibodenberg, not far from the castles of Sponheim and Böckelheim.

Along with Jutta was her relative Hildegard, who at age fourteen was also by now a young marriageable woman.[3] Hildegard had been with Jutta since the age of eight, that is, from the time when she "was given to God for a spiritual life."[4] We may assume that since Hildegard had been dedicated to God at birth, it worked out well for her parents that her relative Jutta took the veil at the age of fourteen (1106). In this way they were able to fulfill their promise by giving their daughter to Sponheim Castle. As was desirable for the sons and daughters of the nobility, Hildegard could also receive a good education there. Jutta, who since early childhood had been instructed by her mother Sophie of Sponheim in reading and transcribing the Scriptures, already had a good education. Unlike noble boys, who had to learn the art of fighting and who only had to read Latin in order learn the virtues of a Christian knight, it was desirable that noble girls should also learn calligraphy and thereby the art of writing in addition to fine craftwork such as embroidery and weaving. Since Jutta, warned by a divine inspiration, now also submitted herself as a disciple for three years to the lady Uda, a widow of Göllheim, who was living in the habit of holy religion, this opportunity also became a chance for Hildegard.[5] It seemed like a good idea to educate both girls together.

The story that eight-year-old Hildegard already had become a recluse "locked away on the hill of St. Disibod," and was even walled in the monastic church in order "to be buried with Christ and to come with him to the glory of the resurrection," was claimed only about fifty years later in her *Vita* in 1180.[6] Following the second and third Lateran Councils (1139 and 1179), this period had brought severe regulations for priests, for instance celibacy, and for monks and nuns, for instance forbidding singing together in the cloister church. "Stability, uniformity, and strict enclosure now represented the ideals for pious women, and the famous prophetess was expected to fit into these ideals. Hildegard and Jutta did not enter the Disibodenberg monastery as proper nuns. This fact was too well known to deny in her biography. But if the *vita* suggested that young Hildegard was walled in as a recluse (there was no argument in favor but also none against it), then the rigorously misogynistic zeitgeist at the end of the 12th century was sufficiently served."[7]

In contrast to this strict zeitgeist of the end of the century, multiple forms of religious life for women had in fact

Disibodenberg ruin site

existed already at the beginning of the twelfth century. Religious women were not simply only nuns. A small incident reported in the *Life of Lady Jutta, Recluse*, written forty years earlier, illustrates this: "There was a certain old woman called Trutwib who was spending the many years of her widowhood like the prophetess Anna in the Gospel, haunting the threshold of the church, and serving the Lord day and night with vigils, fasts and prayers (Luke 2:36-37). This woman had devoutly attended nocturns and lauds on the Kalends of November when the holy festival of All Saints is celebrated. At about sunrise she was going to take a little rest and was returning to the guests' quarters, where the lady Jutta was also staying with her young women on the very day she was to be enclosed."[8]

The *Vita* probably would not have reported about this pious woman Trutwib had she not had a prescient vision of the life and death of Jutta, a vision that would accompany Jutta until the end of her life.

STAGE 5

Disibodenberg – Odernheim on the Glan – Duchroth – Oberhausen on the Nahe – Schloßböckelheim (Böckelheim Castle)

5

Disibodenberg –
Odernheim on the Glan –
Duchroth – Oberhausen on
the Nahe – Schloßböckelheim
(Böckelheim Castle)

Length 15.5 km – ca. 4.5 hrs. – Ascent 330 m – Descent 345 m – medium

In the fifth stage, pilgrims come to the center of the Hildegard Way. Those who have only a day should take their time for a visit to the Disibodenberg. This mountain of volcanic stone has probably been a holy mountain since Celtic and Roman times. As Hildegard of Bingen lived here for nearly forty years (**Tableau 26**), the Disibodenberg represents the

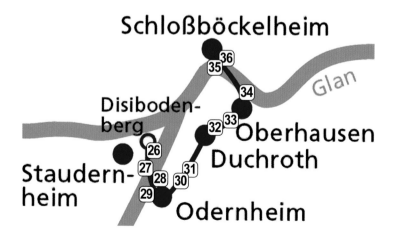

Labyrinth and altar place at the Disibodenberg

spiritual center of the Hildegard Pilgrimage. Many visitors today still seem to sense Hildegard's presence, as Australian poet Colleen Keating describes it in the poem of the day.

The meditation tableau on the topic of the Trinity is to be found at the white Hildegard Chapel that can be seen from afar. Its text stems from Sr. Philippa Rath of Saint Hildegard Abbey (**Tableau 27**). This is remarkable, since Hildegard's vision of the Trinity is also depicted as a huge mosaic decorating the wall of the pilgrimage church in Eibingen, in front of which stands the golden shrine containing the bones of the saint. In this way, the beginning and the end of the Hildegard Way are connected.

The path then leads from the Disibodenberg, possibly down the steep Donkey Path (*Eselspfad*), to the Glan River and to Odernheim where one finds the tableau on the topic of the elements in which Hildegard also describes the water of the Glan (**Tableau 28**).

Historically, we are now in the Bavarian Palatinate, which ecclesiastically is part of the episcopate of Speyer. At a fountain in the center of Odernheim there is a Hildegard sculpture. The next meditation tableau is at the Protestant church (**Tableau 29**, "Baptism").

The pilgrimage path leads us further to a hill with a view of Odernheim and the Disibodenberg from which in particular we can see the white Disibodenberg chapel. Here we find the second meditation corner of the Hildegard Way and a

Along the river to Odernheim

meditation tableau on the topic of confirmation (**Tableau 30**). At the Schlader Heide (heathland), the discovery of a Celtic dwelling with jewelry from the fifth century BC reminds us of the early history of the Naheland; the river still carries its Celtic name, since "Nahe" means "wild river" (**Tableau 31**, "Celtic Homeland").

We walk through the village of Duchroth, which has won several awards as the most beautiful village in Germany and even in Europe. At the end of the circle path (*Ringpfad*) is a small Hildegard Garden (*Hildegardis-Gärtchen*) with the information tableau on healing herbs (**Tableau 19**); at the Protestant church is a further meditation tableau (**Tableau 32**, "Ecclesia and Virginitas"). An open community center and bakery provide the opportunity for a pilgrimage breakfast.

From Duchroth the path guides east along Gangel Mountain to Oberhausen on the Nahe. In front of the Protestant church, we find the next meditation tableau on the topic of Christ and his church (**Tableau 33**). At Luitpold Bridge, facing the Nahe River, the information tableau on fish informs us that

Pilgrimage onto the Disibodenberg now and then

View to the Disibodenberg from the south

Hildegard dedicated herself intensely to studying fish life and the rivers of her environment (**Tableau 34**).

Those who would like to pause before climbing the steep trail to Schloßböckelheim may enjoy a lunch, a coffee or a glass of wine at the "Hermannshöhle," "Gut Herrmannshof" or "Niederthäler Hof." It is still a long way up the site of the ruins of Böckelheim Castle, but the route guides the pilgrim on a wonderful path through the vineyard mountains with a fantastic view of the Nahe valley.

In the twelfth century, Schloßböckelheim, which today appears to be a rather sleepy village, was the site of world history. Here in 1106 (that is, when Hildegard was eight years old), Emperor Henry V imprisoned his own father, Henry IV, for several days in order to force him to abdicate. A merely legendary story tells that Hildegard was born here and encountered Emperor Henry on Christmas Day. This was first claimed by Abbot John Trithemius of Sponheim and then described in poetic terms by local poet Gustav Pfarrius (**Tableau 35**). Even though the huge former castle has been a ruin only since the seventeenth century, from its peak one can still enjoy a great view of the countryside and imagine how the lord or the lady of the castle might have felt there. And one may contemplate a meditation tableau in which Hildegard envisions the powers of evil and their conquest (**Tableau 36**, "The Devil").

POEM

In Search of Hildegard of Bingen

i take a train out of Bingen
through the Rhine Valley
on this summer's day
trek up a steep hill
relieved to find an old sign *klosterruine*
which points to a verdant track
into a cool shady grove
here remnants of the twelfth century monastery
moss-mottled stone walls
mostly buried by vines
and embedded tree roots
is Hildegard's world
standing in this moment
with the outlines of another world
time is shapeless
the divide of centuries a blur
only my mind's eye can see
a spirited young woman
and flourishing herb gardens
she prepares salves and tonics
attends the sick
listens to the breeze
and finds God in the hills above her
kairos time
for her visions writings mandalas and music
later a powerful feminist voice
against corruption
patriarchy and
senseless war
the earth is our mother she would sing

revere and care for her
if we exploit and savage her
she will be out of balance
and the price will be high
then silence for nine hundred years
in our time
the scales are tipped loudly out of balance
measuring life in GDP's
a daily intake of massacres crowds our entertainment
soul mutilation makes soldiers unable to cry
i lean against the wall marked Hildegard's cloister
in the lush shade of an almond tree
hanging fruit voluptuous now
is falling to emptiness
the void
the nothingness
how human to fear the waiting
for fullness to return
scattered around me
are rotting almond fruits
flies enjoying their feast
the decay fodder for the soil
my eyes scan for her presence
a maidenhair fern
grooved into a crumbling niche
catches my eye
delicate and tenacious
I feel a quickening
like a first flutter of new life
too often the fragile
the intimate whisper
the lightness of touch
the flicker of a sanctuary lamp

like breath are portals and easily missed
I ponder the rise and fall of my breathing
listen to the murmur of heart beat
viriditas murmurs Hildegard
Hildegard is here
i do not flinch i expect her
nothing like the grey statue at the abbey
holding the orb and feather
her presence is intimate
light glows luminous
her arms full of herbs from the garden
and her muddy hand-made sandals
make me laugh

Colleen Keating

Rocks on the way to Böckelheim Castle

TABLEAU 26

Hildegard's Time at the Disibodenberg

Disibodenberg

The name of the Disibodenberg derives from the Irish monk St. Disibod, who came into the land of the Nahe River in the seventh century and worked there as a missionary. He probably settled in the ruins of the Villa Rustica, the site of today's Disibodenberger Hof. Around 1100, at the initiative of Archbishop Ruthard of Mainz, Benedictine monks came to the Disibodenberg in order to build a new cloister. After the area was cleared and leveled, the foundation of the new St. Nicholas Church was laid in 1108, and thirty-five years later (in 1143) it was consecrated.

On All Saints Day 1112, three young women were admitted to the monastery on the hill and founded the women's cloister. Double monasteries were quite usual up until the Second Lateran Council, for it meant sharing a comfortable and costly infrastructure. Under the guidance of the twenty-

year-old *magistra* Jutta of Sponheim, fourteen-year-old Hildegard and another young woman entered as well. Hildegard
probably took her vows two years later, in 1114. Upon Jutta's
death in 1136, Hildegard became her successor as *magistra* at
the Disibodenberg.

In her forty-third year, Hildegard received a vision in
which she was called by God to put down everything "she
sees and hears." Supported by the learned monk Volmar, she
began to write down her visions and compose her first visionary work, *Scivias*. The seeress gained fame when it was
reported that Pope Eugene III himself had read publicly from
her work at the Synod of Trier (1147–1148) and had even ordered the Disibodenberg virgin to proceed with her writing.
The women's cloister, which already housed ten sisters at the
time of Jutta's death, attracted more and more postulants and
the space became increasingly tight. Also, after forty years at
the Disibodenberg, Hildegard wished to be active in the world.
Thus, her vision led her to plan and build her own cloister
in Bingen on the Rhine, which she moved into in 1150–1152.
The grave of her teacher Jutta of Sponheim remained at the
Disibodenberg.

TABLEAU 27

The Trinity

Hildegardis Chapel, Disibodenberg

Liber Scivias II.2

PILGRIM'S REFLECTION

What comes to my mind when I think of
the number three?

Why do all good things come in threes?

What do I understand when I hear about
"God the Father, Son and Holy Spirit"?

THE TRINITY

"Then I saw a bright light, and in this light the figure of a man the color of a sapphire, which was all blazing with a gentle glowing fire. And that bright light bathed the whole of the glowing fire, and the glowing fire bathed the bright light; and the bright light and the glowing fire poured over the whole human figure, so that the three were one light in one power of potential."

In the second vision of the second book of *Scivias*, Hildegard reveals to us her vision of the threefold divine secret. No other illumination is as expressive and moving as this vision of the Trinity. Everything here is in motion and full of life. God himself is the wonderful light that gleams and radiates everywhere, the inner power that moves everything, the sparkling fountain of life that pervades the whole universe. In the figure of a man the color of a sapphire, God meets us and looks at us very personally, yet, at the same time, he looks into himself. This is Christ, the Son of God incarnate who is enclosed by the divine light. Lastly, the Holy Spirit is the bright pulsating fire that encircles everything in love. For Hildegard, love is the elemental power that holds together the world and the cosmos and simply everything.

In the beginning was the Word, and the Word was with God, and the Word was God. He was in the beginning with God. All things came into being through him, and without him not one thing came into being. What has come into being in him was life, and the life was the light of all people. The light shines in the darkness, and the darkness did not overcome it. . . .

The true light, which enlightens everyone, was coming into the world. . . .

And the Word became flesh and lived among us, and we have seen his glory, the glory as of a father's only son, full of grace and truth.

John 1:1-5, 9, 14

Laus Trinitati

Laus Trinitati,	To the Trinity be praise!
quae sonus et vita	It is sound and life
ac creatrix omnium in vita	and creator of all beings in
ipsorum est.	their life.
Et quae laus angelicae	It is the praise of the angelic
turbae	host,
et mirus splendor	and the wondrous splendor
arcanorum,	of mysteries
quae hominibus ignota	unknown to humankind:
sunt, est,	
et quae in omnibus vita est.	it is the life in all.

Hildegard of Bingen[1]

TABLEAU 28

Elements

At the Glan River

Liber Physica 2

Air – Water – The Sea – The Lake – The Saar – The Rhine –
The Main – The Danube – The Moselle – The Nahe – The Glan –
Earth – Greenish Earth – Calamine – Chalk

For Hildegard, all of nature is God's creation and it is directed towards serving human beings as the "Crown of Creation." This is also true for elements, already identified in antiquity as fire, water, earth and air. Hildegard sees that "God united the world with four elements, inseparable from each other. The world would not be able to survive if one element could be separated from another. They are indissolubly chained together."

In details, she reflects how these elements work in the human being. They *"quickly make a circuit, like a wheel with its turnings. Fire . . . is in the brain and marrow of a person. . . . The air is in a person's breath and reasoning. . . . The water. . . is in a person's moisture and blood. . . . The earth . . . is in the flesh and bones"* (Hildegard of Bingen, *Causae et Curae*).

In *Physica*, the element of water offers Hildegard an opportunity to examine several rivers. The fact that she describes rivers of her environment may prove that Hildegard as a nun at the Disibodenberg had researched nature and that she may have washed her own face in the nearby river. She writes about the Glan:

*"The **Glan** has its beginning in other rivers, so its water is a bit harsh. It is healthful and useful for food, drink, baths, and face-washing. Its fish are also healthful, but are not long-lived because of the hardness of the water. The sand of the Glan is beautiful and healthful."*

TABLEAU 29

Baptism

Odernheim Protestant Church

Liber Scivias II.3

PILGRIM'S REFLECTION

What does baptism or being baptized
mean to me?

BAPTISM

"After this I saw the image of a woman as large as a great city."

In the third vision of the second book of *Scivias*, Hildegard envisions Ecclesia, the church, as a glorious yet incomplete female figure. At the top right, she embraces God's altar. At the bottom right, we see her as the fisher of men; into the net of her womb she receives dark humans, whom she releases from her mouth, as she says: "I must conceive and give birth!" With the help of God, whom she looks up to, all "her children" receive a pure white garment through baptism. Thereby, she speaks to each one: "Cast off the old injustice and put on the new sanctity." Her children, who are thus baptized, now engage in making music together with Ecclesia (see first section of Vision II.3, p. 142).

As he walked by the sea of Galilee, he saw two brothers, Simon, who is called Peter, and Andrew his brother, casting a net into the sea—for they were fisherman. And he said to them, "Follow me, and I will make you fish for people." Immediately they left their nets and followed him.

Matthew 4:18-20

SONG

O orzchis Ecclesia

O orzchis (immensa)
   Ecclesia,
armis divinis praecincta,
et hyacintho ornata,
tu es caldemia (aroma)
stigmatum loifolum
   (populorum)
et urbs scientiarum.
O, o, tu es etiam crizanta
   (uncta)
in alto sono,
et es chorzta (corusca)
   gemma.

O measureless Church,

girded with divine armor
and adorned with jacinth,
you are the fragrance
of the wounds of nations,

the city of sciences.
O, o you are anointed

amid lofty song:
you are a sparkling gem.

Hildegard of Bingen[2]

TABLEAU 30

Confirmation

Meditation Corner

Liber Scivias II.4

PILGRIM'S REFLECTION

Who or what gives me support and
encouragement in my life?

What ointments and anointments
are good for me?

What does confirmation mean to me?

_____

_____

_____

_____

_____

_____

_____

_____

_____

_____

_____

_____

_____

_____

_____

CONFIRMATION

"And then I saw the image of an immense round tower, all made of a single white stone."

In the fourth vision of the second book of *Scivias*, Hildegard envisions the female figure of Ecclesia, the church, in front of an immense round tower; from its upper three windows shines much brilliance. This is the "anointing of the Holy Spirit" that flows to Ecclesia's children in their confirmation in order to strengthen them in their life.

> My speech and my proclamation were not with plausible words of wisdom, but with a demonstration of the Spirit and of power, so that your faith might rest not on human wisdom but on the power of God.
>
> 1 Corinthians 2:4-5

SONG

De Spiritu Sancto—O Fire of the Spirit

O ignis Spiritus Paracliti,

vita vitae omnis creaturae,
sanctus es vivificando
* formas.*
Sanctus es ungendo
* periculose fractos,*
sanctus es tergendo fetida
* vulnera.*

O spiraculum sanctitatis,
o ignis caritatis,
o dulcis gustus in
* pectoribus*
et infusio cordium
in bono odore virtutum.

O fons purrissimus,
in quo consideratur,
quod Deus alienos colligit
et perditos requirit.

O fire of the Spirit, the
  Comforter,
life of the life of all creation,
holy are you, giving life to
  the forms.
Holy are you, anointing the
  dangerously broken;
holy are you, cleansing the
  fetid wounds.

O breath of sanctity,
O fire of charity,
O sweet savor in the breast

and balm flooding hearts
with the fragrance of virtues.

O limpid fountain,
in which it is seen
how God gathers the strays
and seeks out the lost.

Hildegard of Bingen[3]

TABLEAU 31

Celtic Homeland

Schlader Heide

"St. Disibod," sculpture by Paul Seitz

On the Hildegard Way, we are in the old homeland of the Celts or in *Gallia* (Gaul). The site where we are standing, the Schlader Heide, was an old Celtic settlement place. As a scenic monument, the Disibodenberg, situated between the Glan and Nahe Rivers, has most likely been a "holy mountain," that is, a cult place, not only since the Roman period but already in Celtic times.

In the seventh century, the Gaelic-speaking Irish monk St. Disibod came to Frankish Gaul and set up his beehive cell at the site that was shown to him in a vision, namely *"where green leaves sprout from his walking stick, where a white hind with her hoofs scratches a well of fresh water from the earth and where two rivers unite."*

Hildegard of Bingen, of whom it is reported in her *Vita* that she was born in Gaul, wrote the *vita* of the Gaelic saint Disibod after whom the holy mountain is named today.

But who were the Celts? According to Greek and Roman historiography, with evidence provided by archeological excavations of many hill graves and settlements, the Celts lived in the low mountain range between Bohemia and northeast France at least since the seventh century BC. They are described as having a light skin, a tall figure, impressive in physical appearance and in their cloth, as well as striking with awe as warriors. The Celtic tribe of the Treverians whose name was given to the city of Trier by the Romans (*Augusta Trevorum*), lived in the region west of the Rhine up to present-day Luxembourg.

The land of the Celts was characterized by residences of princes and a rich trade with the Mediterranean area. There was a Celtic city at the Donnersberg. Near Bundenbach, houses of a Celtic settlement, the Altburg, were reconstructed. One of the richest "princess graves" with golden jewelry and bronze drinking vessels was found in Waldalgesheim. And even today there is a Celtic message in the name of the Nahe River: it derives from the Celtic word *nava*, which means "wild river."

TABLEAU 32

Ecclesia and Virginitas

Duchroth Protestant Church

Liber Scivias II.5

PILGRIM'S REFLECTION

What image do I have of the church?

What should the ideal church look like?

ECCLESIA AND VIRGINITAS

"After this I saw that a splendor white as snow and trans-lucent as crystal had shone around the image of that woman from the top of her head to her throat."

In the fifth vision of the second book of *Scivias*, Hildegard envisions the female figure of Ecclesia, the Church. Her lower body is a strong, firm rock and the upper part of her body shows the gesture of a blessing priestess (orant). In her heart stands Virginitas, the female figure of virginity. For Hildegard, she represents utter surrender and orientation towards God. In this way, she associates virginity (*virginitas*) with virtue (*virtus*) and also with viridity (*viriditas*). All three are Hildegard's ideals for the church that she sees as a mystical body.

For just as the body is one and has many members, and all the members of the body, though many, are one body, so it is with Christ. For in the one Spirit we were all baptized into one body—Jews or Greeks, slaves or free—and we were all made to drink of one Spirit. . . .

[T]he members of the body that seem to be weaker are indispensable, and those members of the body that we think less honorable we clothe with greater honor, and our less respectable members are treated with greater respect; whereas our more respectable members do not need this. But God has so arranged the body, giving the greater honor to the inferior member, that there may be no dissension within the body, but the members may have the same care for one another. . . .

Now you are the body of Christ and individually members of it. And God has appointed in the church first apostles, second prophets, third teachers; then deeds of power, then gifts of healing, forms of assistance, forms of leadership, various kinds of tongues.

1 Corinthians 12:12-13, 22-26, 27-28

TABLEAU 33

Christ and His Church

Oberhausen Protestant Church

Liber Scivias II.6

What is Christ's sacrifice for me?

What does it mean to me to receive bread and wine at communion or Eucharist?

_____

_____

_____

_____

_____

_____

_____

_____

_____

_____

_____

_____

_____

_____

_____

_____

_____

CHRIST AND HIS CHURCH

"And after these things I saw the Son of God hanging on the cross, and the aforementioned image of a woman coming forth like a bright radiance from the ancient counsel."

In the sixth vision of the second book of *Scivias*, Hildegard envisions the female figure of Ecclesia, the church, as she receives the Blood of Christ in her chalice during his crucifixion and stands as a priestess at his high altar. The biblical testimony of the passion, death and resurrection is illuminated in the background. For Hildegard, the moment of "Christ's sacrifice," in which he pours out his blood, represents the "Wedding on Mount Calvary." In this wedding between Christ and his church, she receives her most precious treasure of the Body and Blood of Christ which, which she can hand out from now on. Therefore, this is Hildegard's vision of the sacrament of the Eucharist.

When it was evening, he came with the twelve. . . .

While they were eating, he took a loaf of bread, and after blessing it he broke it, gave it to them, and said, "Take; this is my body." Then he took a cup, and after giving thanks he gave it to them, and all of them drank from it. He said to them, "This is my blood of the covenant, which is poured out for many. Truly I tell you, I will never again drink of the fruit of the vine until that day when I drink it new in the kingdom of God."

Mark 14:17, 22-25

SONG

O virgo Ecclesia

O virgo Ecclesia,
plangendum est,
quod saevissimus lupus
filios tuos de latere tuo
    abstraxit.
O vae callido serpenti!
Sed o quam pretiosus est

sanguis Salvatoris,
qui in vexillo Regis

Ecclesiam ipsi desponsavit,
unde filios illius requirit.

O virgin Church,
we must grieve
because a most savage wolf
has snatched your children
    from your side.
O woe to the cunning serpent!
But O how precious is the
    blood
of the Savior,
who betrothed the Church to
    himself
with the King's standard.
Therefore he is seeking her
    children.

Hildegard of Bingen[4]

159

TABLEAU 34

Fish

Oberhausen on the Nahe

Liber Physica 5

Whale – Dolphin – Sturgeon – Turbot – Salmon – Sheatfish –
Pike – Copprea – Northern Pike – European Catfish – Carp –
Sea Bream – Elsua – Plaice – Salmon Trout – Monuwa – Perch –
Meysisch – A fish having a shell – Roach – Grayling – Herring –
Groundling – Chub – Bleak – Pafenduno – Tench – Grundula –
Stechela – Loach – Rulheubt – Crawfish – Eel – Cod –
Punbelen – Lamprey

Hildegard wrote about no other animal as elaborately as
she did about fish. Even though the fifth book of *Physica* con-
siders "fish" that Hildegard probably never saw, such as the
whale, which is important in the Biblical narrative (Book of
Jonah), most fish that she examines are nevertheless freshwa-
ter fish of her nearby environment that were a major source of
nourishment in her time. Thereby, she has observed so many

details about fish life in the nearby Nahe and Glan Rivers that she can be called a natural researcher.

"Certain fish live naturally at the bottom of the sea and rivers. They furrow the sea bottom, just as pigs furrow the earth, and there they eat roots of certain plants. They live a long time on these and other suitable foods which they seek out. They sometimes ascend almost to the middle of those waters and sometimes go down to the bottom, where they dwell."

In *Physica*, Hildegard talks about the use and the healing effect of eating fish. Thus, she finds that healthy people can or should eat sturgeon, trout, roach, chub, bleak or *pafenduno*. For ill people, she recommends salmon for teeth problems, sheatfish for eye problems, northern pike for digestion problems, carp and sea bream for fever, *elusa* for strengthening the heart and herring for cleansing abscesses.

TABLEAU 35

Böckelheim Castle

Ruin site

Böckelheim Castle. Etching by Matthäus Merian, 1645.

Böckelheim Castle was one of the oldest and most important castles in the Nahe area. In a document of Louis the Pious from 824, a "villa Beccchilenheim" is mentioned. The position on a mountain above the Nahe River was of strategic value. Böckelheim was the center of the region. The castle was owned by the dukes of Swabia and from Lorraine; in 1046, it was besieged and destroyed by King Henry III.

In 1101, the reconstructed castle was in the possession of the bishopric of Speyer, which in turn gave it as a fief to the Earls of Sponheim. The loss of the castle to the archbishopric of Mainz caused the battle of Sprendlingen, which was won by the archbishop's troops. The story goes that in this battle the butcher Michel Mort saved Earl John from imprisonment by sacrificing his own life.

There are hardly any remains from this once imposing castle. Recognizable elements include a piece of the fortified tower in the ring of the upper castle, part of the protective wall, a little corner tower of the outer bailey and some remaining parts of the wall's ring. The huge fortress that is shown in an etching by Matthäus Merian the Elder was destroyed in 1688 by the troops of Louis XIV of France.

Böckelheim Castle became famous because at Christmas 1105, King Henry IV was imprisoned there for some days by his own son, the later king Henry V, in order to force him to resign. Abbot John Trithemus claimed that Böckelheim was the birthplace of Hildegard of Bingen. This is not supported by historical research today.

Gustav Pfarrius, a poet from nearby Guldental, mentions in his collection of poems, *Das Nahetal in Bildern* (The Nahe valley in images; 1838), little Hildegard as the daughter of the lord of the castle who encounters the emperor and prays for the ex-communicated one. This is a sympathetic poetic invention.

Michael Vesper

Then Jesus was led up by the Spirit into the wilderness to be tempted by the devil. He fasted forty days and forty nights, and afterwards he was famished. The tempter came and said to him, "If you are the Son of God, command these stones to become loaves of bread." But he answered, "It is written, 'One does not live by bread alone, but by every word that comes from the mouth of God.'" Then the devil took him to the holy city and placed him on the pinnacle of the temple, saying to him, "If you are the Son of God, throw yourself down; for it is written, 'He will command his angels concerning you,' and 'On their hands they will bear you up, so that you will not dash your foot against a stone.'" Jesus said to him, "Again it is written, 'Do not put the Lord your God to the test.'" Again, the devil took him to a very high mountain and showed him all the kingdoms of the world and their splendor; and he said to him, "All these I will give you, if you will fall down and worship me." Jesus said to him, "Away with you, Satan! for it is written, 'Worship the Lord your God, and serve only him.'" Then the devil left him, and suddenly angels came and waited on him.

Matthew 4:1-11

TABLEAU 36

The Devil

Böckelheim Castle Ruins

Liber Scivias II.7

What image of the "devil" do I have?

What do I think about "the evil" in this world?

What can I do myself in order to make the world a better place?

THE DEVIL

In the seventh and last vision of the second book of *Scivias*, Hildegard envisions "a monster shaped like a worm, wondrously large and long, which aroused an indescribable sense of horror and rage . . . "

It is lying in chains on the ground. Flames, sharp arrows and a foul-smelling vapor still emanate from its mouth; and so humans who come too close can still be hurt. All of the baptized (at the top of the image) are grateful that the 'malicious serpent' is now chained at its neck, hands and feet and thereby tamed. However, the battle against the devil, against evil in the world and in ourselves has to go on; it is everyone's task. Hildegard envisions:

"But behold, a great multitude of people came, shining brightly; they forcefully trod the worm underfoot and severely tormented it, but could not be injured by its flames or its poison."

King Henry's Christmas

The emperor—imprisoned!
The trap had been well laid;
The son had his own father
Despicably betrayed.

The Nahe, ever-rolling
Has washed the stones since then,
But still the Castle Böckelheim
Has never been washed clean.

He sat without complaining,
He sat with staring glance,
As Christmastide came nearer,
He sat as in a trance.

His curls still decorated
His once so noble face,
But every mark of courage
Had vanished without trace.

"What sin has he committed —
This strange and silent man?"
Asked Hildegard the child,
As best a child can.

She felt a deep compassion
Though tender yet in years,
Thus Hildebert's young sister,
Was full of kindly tears.

"What heartbreak is he feeling,
This man, so silently:
As he looks through his tears at
My brother and at me?"

"My child," said her mother,
"On his head heavily lies
The church's wrath; so for him,
The fount of grace is dry."

The daughter crossed herself
And hurried back to say,
"O Mother, I will pray for him,
Right now, without delay!"
And knelt before the prisoner
Who trembled there in pain.

And so above the castle
That Christmas came and went;
The father stayed a captive,
The son would not relent.

The emperor was threatened
With death, till, beaten down,
In deep humiliation
He offered up his crown.

Gustav Pfarrius
Translated by Ruth B. Griffoen

Third Station in Hildegard's Life: Almost Forty Years at the Disibodenberg

by Annette Esser

Hildegard lived for many years at Disibodenberg without revealing the strange and confusing experience of her "showings" or "visions." Only Jutta must have known something about them, or at least was aware of Hildegard's special gift, for Hildegard was the *"certain faithful disciple of Lady Jutta herself, one who had been on the most intimate terms with her"*[5]. According to her *Vita*, *"Jutta carefully fitted her for a garment of humility and innocence, and, instructed her in the songs of David, showed her how to play the ten-stringed psaltery"*; in other words she taught her to understand and sing in Latin.[6] And then there was Volmar, the learned monk who was about Hildegard's age, to whom her further education was entrusted and who became her lifelong friend, confidant and secretary.

The fact that Hildegard did not study theology in a modern sense needs to be understood in the context of her time, the twelfth century. Before Pope Gregory decreed in 1079 that schools were to be established at the great cathedrals and before the first universities were founded in the thirteenth century, monasteries held a monopoly on education and culture. In other words, in early medieval society, monks both maintained and transferred the knowledge of antiquity, which had been kept and conveyed from the ancient church through the early Middle Ages, which were dark ages in this region. Thus, in her time, Hildegard was at an excellent place for pre-scholastic education and theological learning; in spite of all her humble pronouncements of being an "unlearned woman," it needs to be said that *magistra* Jutta and *magistra* Hildegard, as they were called, were highly learned women. And Volmar was the learned monk at their side who had mastery of the seven liberal arts, including Latin grammar and the writing of musical notes, called neumes.

During her time at the Disibodenberg, Hildegard took part in the Benedictine life of the double monastery: praying the Liturgy of the Hours and singing psalms in the monastic church; attending High Mass on feast days; taking care of the cloister gardens; studying the scriptures (in the *Vulgate*); and sometimes even receiving visits from dignitaries:

In 1120, after the relics of Saint Ursula were discovered in Cologne, some of them were brought to the Disibodenberg (dividing the relics of one saint's body was a common practice). Saint Ursula, who together with her 11,000 virgins bravely defended her virginity against the Huns, was a role model for Hildegard and probably her favorite saint. Thus, in honor of her she composed an entire mass for her feast day:

> *In visione vere fidei Ursula filium Dei amavit et virum cum hoc seculo reliquit et solem in aspexit . . .* / Ursula fell in love with God's Son in a vision: her faith was true. She rejected her man and the world and gazed straight into the sun.[7]

In 1138 Bishop Sigward of Uppsala, Sweden, came and consecrated three side altars and one altar in the main choir. The film "Vision" depicts that on the visit he also brought his "travel library" with some valuable books by Greek philosophers and Arab physicians, which Hildegard could study.

In 1143 Archbishop Henry of Mainz dedicated the main monastery church and its high altar to Saint John, who was understood at the time to be at once Jesus' beloved disciple, apostle, evangelist and apocalyptic seer. When she later referred to herself later as the "trumpet of God" (Rev 1:10) and as the "eagle," Hildegard identified very much with John:

Ah, ah eagle, why do you sleep on in your knowledge? Rise up from your hesitancy.[8]

In the same year 1143, the relics of St. Disibod were ceremonially buried in the tomb of the monastery church. Thirty years later, at the request of Abbot Helenger and the monks of Disibodenberg, Hildegard wrote the saint's *vita*. (1170).

Thus, Hildegard experienced and learned much in her nearly forty years at the Disibodenberg. All the knowledge that she wrote down years later in Latin about stones, plants and animals, as well as their meaning and healing power for humans, must have been acquired during this time. And yet, her knowledge is not confined to traditional monastic medicine. Rather we may recognize that Hildegard was a natural researcher with a thirst for knowledge beyond the monastic walls. For example, she observed intensively the life of fish in the nearby Glan River, the flight of the birds in the air and the behavior of animals on land. We may also recognize how Hildegard must have studied the medical works of ancient and Arabic authors in the large monastic library, even though she does not quote these sources. Still, Hildegard's writings seem too original to be reduced to the sources studied in the history of medicine. The assumption of many Hildegard friends—that Hildegard also must have sensed or felt spiritually in some way which particular plants could be a healing remedy for which particular illnesses—is also the basis of today's Hildegard medicine; even if the assumption that Hildegard was only an "inspired vessel" who received her knowledge solely through her visions "in a direct dictation from God"[9] cannot be defended any more.

In the course of time, the women's cell developed into a Benedictine women's convent. The extraordinary fame of Lady Jutta attracted ten more women as postulants. When Jutta died on December 22, 1136, just before Christmas, Hildegard was elected as her successor, which had been the wish of the deceased. Now, everybody expected that the new *magistra* would walk "in Jutta's footsteps" and perhaps also become like her. Jutta had a "caring heart" and had maintained many personal contacts and had exchanged letters with people of all classes. But what not everybody could see was that Jutta had imposed a very strict form of asceticism on herself,

in vigils, praying and continual fasting, in cold and nakedness (2 Cor. 11:27). Among the various ways in which she inflicted relentless torments and wounds to her body she wore a hair-shirt and an iron chain, by means of which she had already been accustomed to subduing her youthful limbs.[10]

How much she had been torturing her body only became fully visible to her confidant Hildegard after her death, when she had to wash Jutta's body with two other sisters:

"These disciples of hers, watering the body of their mother and magistra with heartfelt tears, carefully examined it. Among innumerable other marks of her passion they discovered that a chain which she had worn on her flesh had made three furrows right around her body."[11]

STAGE 6

Schloßböckelheim (Böckelheim Castle) – Waldböckelheim – Burgsponheim – Sponheim – Braunweiler

6

Schloßböckelheim (Böckelheim Castle) – Waldböckelheim – Burgsponheim – Sponheim – Braunweiler

Length 14.2 km – ca. 4 hrs. – Ascent 363 m – Descent 236 m – medium

From Böckelheim Castle, the path leads two kilometers downhill to the small town of Waldböckelheim. At St. Bartholomäus Catholic Church, which also contains a Hildegard relic, we find the first meditation tableau of the third book of *Scivias*; it tells us about the cosmic drama that took place at the beginning of time according to Hildegard (**Tableau 37**). Near the old barn for collecting the tithe (*Zehntscheune*), an information reminds us that Hildegard was dedicated to God as

Monstrance with relic of
St. Hildegard in St. Bartholomäus
Church in Waldböckelheim

a "tithe" (**Tableau 38**). In order to look at the second meditation tableau about Hildegard's concept of the City of God, we need to climb the hill of the nineteenth-century Protestant church which can be seen in the countryside from afar (**Tableau 39**).

From there, the Hildegard Way moves clearly away from the west-east direction to Bad Kreuznach, the biggest town in the Nahe valley, and further north into the Hunsrück mountains. The reason for this change of direction is that we want to move to the historic Hildegard sites that connect to her teacher, Jutta of Sponheim, and her family, the earls of Sponheim, who governed this whole region up to the fifteenth century.

After a walk of two kilometers, we arrive in Burgsponheim.

A visit to the castle ruins invites us to rest and remember the history of Jutta and Hildegard. From Hildegard's *Vita* we know that she was brought to Jutta at the age of eight and was thereby "offered to God for a spiritual life." We also know that Hildegard did not come at that time to the Disibodenberg, for she and Jutta only entered there at the age of fourteen and twenty respectively; rather, she probably came here to Sponheim Castle, where Jutta's family lived. Here we find an information tableau about Hildegard's teacher, Jutta of Sponheim, whose life was shaped by the strict reform movements

On the way to Sponheim Castle and
Sponheim Minster

of her time (**Tableau 40**). We also find a meditation tableau on
the "Tower of Anticipation" (**Tableau 41**), which inspired the
poem of the day. It invites us to listen to Hildegard's favorite
song "O virga ac diadema."

Through fields and forest, the Hildegard Way guides us 1.5
kilometers further to Sponheim; with its important minster,
which can already be seen from afar.

Sponheim Minster is important for the Hildegard Way as
it is the only remaining building from Hildegard's epoch, the
twelfth century (**Tableau 43**). It is also important because of
Abbot John Trithemius of Sponheim (1462–1516), who lived
here and who, as a humanist, wrote on Hildegard of Bingen,
whom he venerated and to whose fame he crucially contributed. Even though his historical statements, for example about
Böckelheim Castle being Hildegard's birthplace, were not
correct, his writings on Hildegard were accepted unques-
tioned as a historical source in all Hildegard literature until
the twentieth century.

Here the pilgrim can also look at the meditation tableau on
the "Pillar of the Word of God" (**Tableau 42**). And those who
would like to stay a little bit more can take time for a walking
meditation through the labyrinth, enjoy a concert under the
domed roof of the minster or observe the further activities of

176

Sponheim Minster

this special site, which is becoming an important center of the whole Hildegard Way.

Energetic pilgrims who do not want to stay in Sponheim overnight can walk three kilometers further to Braunweiler. In the late evening one may also choose to drive, for there are no more additional Hildegard tableaux until Braunweiler.

The text of the day is about one more station in Hildegard's life, namely, the interesting story as to how she gained fame in the whole medieval world with the revelation of her visions.

On the Hildegard pilgrimage

TABLEAU 37

God, Lucifer, and Humanity

St. Bartholomäus Catholic Church

Liber Scivias III.1

PILGRIM'S REFLECTION

Have I ever thought about what there was when the universe did not yet exist?

What do I connect with light and darkness, physically and psychologically?

"And I, a person . . . I looked towards the East. And there I saw a single block of stone . . . and a white cloud above it; and above the cloud a royal throne . . . on which One was sitting. . . . He held to his breast what looked like black and filthy mire, as big as a human heart, surrounded with precious stones and pearls."

In this first vision of the third book of *Scivias,* Hildegard visualizes the great cosmic drama; this took place before the beginning of times, in heaven as well as in the underworld, and led to the creation of the human being. Thus, she envisions a huge star with much radiance and beauty emanating from the almighty God enthroned in the East. This is Lucifer, who is a creature of God, like all angels. Since he desires to be like God, he moves to the maximum distance from God and, together with his fellows, he plunges towards the North into utter darkness. God takes the remaining blaze of light and attaches it to the clump of clay that he lovingly holds to His heart. By this, God forms his second creature, the human being.

Praise the LORD with the lyre; / make melody to him with the harp of ten strings. . . . / For the word of the LORD is upright, / and all his work is done in faithfulness. / He loves righteousness and justice; / the earth is full of the steadfast love of the LORD. / By the word of the LORD the heavens were made, / and all their host by the breath of his mouth. . . . / The counsel of the LORD stands forever, / the thoughts of his heart to all generations. . . . / From where he sits enthroned he watches / all the inhabitants of the earth— / he who fashions the hearts of them all, / and observes all their deeds. . . . / Truly the eye of the LORD is on those who fear him, / on those who hope in his steadfast love, / to deliver their soul from death, / and to keep them alive in famine. / Our soul waits for the LORD; / he is our help and shield. / Our heart is glad in him, / because we trust in his holy name. / Let your steadfast love, O LORD, be upon us, / even as we hope in you.

Psalm 33:2, 4-6, 11, 14-15, 18-22

TABLEAU 38

The Tithe

Waldböckelheim, near the Old Tithe Barn

"All tithes from the land, whether the seed from the ground or the fruit from the tree, are the LORD's; they are holy to the LORD." (Leviticus 27:30)

Mosaic law demanded that the people of Israel pay in kind a tithe of their harvest in order to support the priests and assist the poor. Also, in early Christianity, the tithe was postulated as a moral duty. In Hildegard's time, the taking of the tithe had become a legal right of the church. As a result, it was possible to build churches, maintain the clerics, provide relief for the poor and, all in all, to become a wealthy institution.

Whoever could not or did not want to deliver the tithe had to fear heavy sanctions that could even extend to excommunication, which in the homogeneous medieval society amounted to a death sentence. Except for clerics and monasteries that were exempt, everyone had to pay the tithe. There was a distinction between the large tithe that included grains and wine and various small tithes: the green tithe pertained to vegetables, fruits and other products of the fields and gardens and the blood tithe involved animals and animal products (wool, lamb, milk).

In Waldböckelheim, Sobernheim, Nussbaum, Monzingen and Schloßböckelheim, originally the lord of the tithe was the bishopric of Speyer and then, beginning with the battle of Sprendlingen in 1279, the Mainz bishopric. The current tithe barn in Waldböckelheim was built according to a design from 1740 and shows the sign of the Mainz bishopric: the Mainz wheel.

How deeply rooted the duty to pay the tithe was in religious consciousness is also shown in the life story of Hildegard of Bingen (1098–1179). We are told that Hildegard was the tenth child of noble parents who dedicated her "while sighing" to God as a tithe. In her time, this form of consecration was not unusual and Hildegard accepted it for herself. Yet, later in life, she disapproved of consecration without one's own will.

Michael Vesper

TABLEAU 39

The Edifice of Salvation

Walsböckelheim Protestant Church

Liber Scivias III.2

What do the four directions—east, north, west and south—mean geophysically and symbolically?

Where have I already built up something in my life and, what have I experienced and learned from it?

_____

_____

_____

_____

_____

_____

_____

_____

_____

_____

_____

_____

THE EDIFICE OF SALVATION

"Then I saw, within the circumference of the circle, which ex-tended from the One seated on the throne, a great mountain. . . . And on that mountain stood a four-sided building, formed in the likeness of a four-walled city. . . . One of its corners faced the East, one faced the West, one the North and one the South."

In this second vision of the third book of *Scivias*, Hildegard envisions the construction of a whole city, something that she saw practically all of her cloistered life at the construction sites of the Disibodenberg and the Rupertsberg. This is the City of God whose foundation has been set by God in the East. From there, this city grows to the North on the left side into the darkness and "oblivion of God"; further to the West into the sunset and "shadow of death"; further to the South, where Christ rises as the "sun of justice"; and, it closes again in the East, where the "origin of justice" is and where finally the "day of revelation" will take place. Since the time of incarnation, the walls of this city have been half built. Now, it is the task for humans to further build up this city in co-operation with the Divine architect until the end of times.

Then one of the seven angels . . . came. . . . And in the spirit he carried me away to a great, high mountain and showed me the holy city Jeru-salem coming down out of heaven from God. It has the glory of God and a radiance like a very rare jewel, like jasper, clear as crystal. It has a great, high wall with twelve gates, and at the gates twelve angels, and on the gates are inscribed the names of the twelve tribes of the Israelites; on the east three gates, on the north three gates, on the south three gates, and on the west three gates. And the wall of the city has twelve foundations, and on them are the twelve names of the twelve apostles of the Lamb.

The angel who talked to me had a measuring rod of gold to measure the city and its gates and walls.

Revelation 21:9-15

SONG

O magne Pater

O magne Pater,
in magna necessitate sumus.
Nunc igitur obsecramus,
obsecramus te per Verbum tuum,
per quod nos constituisti
plenos quibus indigemus.

Nunc placeat tibi, Pater,
quia te decet,
ut aspicias in nos per adiutorium tuum,
ut non deficiamus,
et ne nomen tuum in nobis obscuretur,
et per ipsum nomen tuum dignare nos adiuvare.

Great Father,
we are in great need!
Now then we beseech,
we beseech you by your Word,
through which you created us full
of the things we lack.

Now, Father, may it please you,
for it befits you,
to look upon us and help us,
that we may not perish,
that your name be not darkened within us:
and by your own name, graciously help us.

Hildegard of Bingen[1]

TABLEAU 40

Jutta of Sponheim

Sponheim Castle

"How St. Hildegard came to St. Jutta onto
the Disibodenberg." Fresco in St. Hildegard's Abbey.

In 1092 AD, Jutta of Sponheim was born in Burgsponheim
as the daughter of Earl Stephan II and Sophia of Formbach.
Her younger brother, Hugo of Sponheim, was Archbishop of
Cologne for a short time. After the early death of her father,
when Jutta was three years old, her older brother, Meinhard
of Sponheim, became his successor. The widowed mother,
Sophia, took care of the good education of her daughter.

During a serious illness at the age of twelve, Jutta vowed
to become a nun if she survived. And in fact, from then on, she
refused all proposals of marriage, and, against the will of her
family, she took the veil from Ruthard, Archbishop of Mainz,
and dedicated her life to God. To this end, she subordinated

herself for three years as a student to the widow Uda of Göl-heim, who "lived in the habit of the holy religion."

As Hildegard, according to her *Vita*, came to Jutta at the age of eight (1106), we can assume that Jutta and Hildegard received together religious education from the pious widow. After the death of her mother, Jutta wanted to go on a pilgrimage to the Holy Land. This time, her brother Meinhard interfered and arranged for his sister to enter the newly founded Disibodenberg monastery.

On November 1, 1112, Jutta made the vow of monastic life to Abbot Burchard of Disibodenberg and was accepted as a recluse along with two other virgins, one of whom was Hildegard. With Jutta of Sponheim as the first *magistra*, the Disibodenberg women's cell was founded.

To the outside world, Jutta appeared as a friendly and learned woman who had many contacts and was much liked. Yet, in the spirit of the reform movements of her time, she lived a strict ascetic life that did not merely include rigorous fasting but also self-flagellation and wearing an iron belt. Jutta directed the women's cell until her death on December 22, 1136. Hildegard became Jutta's successor as the second *magistra* at the Disibodenberg.

TABLEAU 41

The Tower of Anticipation

At the Tower of Sponheim Castle

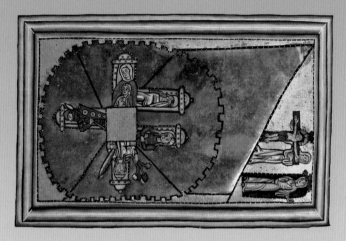

Liber Scivias III.3

If there were no religious rules or
commandments, would we still be able to
recognize what is good and what is bad or evil?

What ethical attitudes do I strive for in my life?

THE TOWER OF ANTICIPATION

"After this I looked, and behold! In the middle of the shining part of the building's outer wall there stood an iron-colored tower. . . . In it I saw five figures."

In this third vision of the third book of *Scivias*, Hildegard envisions the "Tower of Anticipation of God's will" as the first building of the City of God. It is at the northeastern wall of mirror-like knowledge (of good and evil) that connects the time of Noah, Abraham and Moses. Thus, this is about the character and attitudes that all humans of good will can acquire even before the revelation of the New Testament. Hildegard envisions—down from the middle and counterclockwise—the love of heavenly things (*amor caelestis*), discipline (*disciplina*), shamefacedness (*verecundia*), mercy (*misericordia*) and victory (*victoria*). Facing the tower to the right are two more figures: the one above with the cross is desire (*desiderium*) and the one below is patience (*patientia*).

Praise the LORD with the lyre; / make melody to him with the harp of ten strings. / Sing to him a new song; / play skillfully on the strings, with loud shouts. / For the word of the LORD is upright, / and all his work is done in faithfulness. / He loves righteousness and justice; / the earth is full of the steadfast love of the LORD. / By the word of the LORD the heavens were made, / and all their host by the breath of his mouth. . . . / For he spoke, and it came to be; / he commanded, and it stood firm. / The LORD brings the counsel of the nations to nothing; / he frustrates the plans of the peoples. / The counsel of the LORD stands forever, / the thoughts of his heart to all generations.

Psalm 33:2-6, 9-11

POEM

This Is What I Wish For

Love for heavenly as well as earthly things

Wholesome discipline that does not make me sick
but rather gives me freedom

The protecting veil of shame that keeps my dignity

Understanding mercy

To win the battle against the addictions in my life

Patience with myself and with others

And in my life never to lose the desire for you, o God.

Amen

Annette Esser

TABLEAU 42

The Pillar of the Word of God

Sponheim Minster

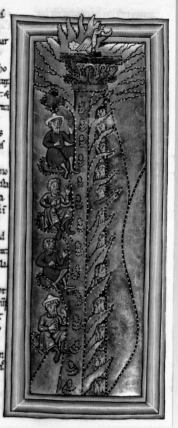

Liber Scivias III.4

PILGRIM'S REFLECTION

What is the "Word of God," and what does it
mean to me?

What characters from the Bible or from the history
of Christianity are important to me and why?

_____

_____

_____

_____

_____

_____

_____

_____

_____

_____

_____

_____

THE PILLAR OF THE WORD OF GOD

"And then, beyond the tower . . . I saw a pillar."

In this fourth vision of the third book of *Scivias*, Hildegard envisions a pillar with three sides. Some important figures of the Old and New Testament as well as of church history thus far are sitting on it. On the left side from the base upwards these are Abraham, Moses, Joshua, and the other patriarchs and prophets of the Old Testament. To the right, Hildegard envisions apostles, martyrs, confessors, virgins, and saints of Christianity. The silver-shaped form on the third side hints at the development of biblical exegesis by the church fathers over the course of history. Above all, on the pillar, is enthroned the dove of the Holy Spirit.

Pilgrims climbing the stairs to Sponheim Minster

The word of God continued to spread; the number of the disciples increased greatly in Jerusalem.

Acts 6:7

TABLEAU 43

Sponheim Minster

In the twelfth century, the earls of Sponheim founded the minster (*Klosterkirche*) of the same name. According to the chronicle written by Abbot John Trithemius (1462–1516), it was Earl Meinhard, brother of Jutta of Sponheim, who founded the monastery in 1124. However, the historical credibility is questionable. The earls were reeves, that is, worldly reeves; the spiritual custody was incumbent on the bishop of Mainz. The monastery of St. Alban and St. Jacob was settled initially by twelve monks and a number of *conversi*, servants that were under the rule. There were never more than twenty monks; during Trithemius' time, there were only five.

The former minster and today's St. Mary and St. Martin Catholic Church has a Greek cross as a ground plan because the nave was never built out. The choir, the transept with the apses, as well as the columns with the corresponding pointed arches of the crossing are Romanesque in style.

John Trithemius was the most well-known abbot of Sponheim monastery. He intended to reform the monastic life and, as a humanistic scholar, he built up the huge library that made Sponheim a center for scholars. Because of internal conflicts he had to leave Sponheim and became the abbot of Würzburg. In his historical writings, he always refers to Hildegard of Bingen, whom he venerated. It was Trithemius who crucially contributed to her posthumous fame. Many of his assertions, however, such as Böckelheim Castle being the place of her birth, are inventions or falsifications.

The monastery itself was closed in the course of the Reformation; later it was founded anew and in 1803 it was finally secularized.

Michael Vesper

Fourth Station in Hildegard's Life: The "Revelation" of *Liber Scivias*

by Annette Esser

Hildegard was thirty-eight years old when she became the second *magistra* at the Disibodenberg after Jutta's death. Jutta's ideal, combining public friendliness with physical punishment of her own body, did not seem to be what Hildegard wanted to make her own. In addition, she did not use her authority immediately to reveal her visions.

The *Vita* reports that instead she refrained from this "out of female shyness, out of the fear that people would talk and of the harsh judgment of humans." Only five years later, "the time drew near for her life and teaching to be displayed for the benefit of many. . . . She was constrained by a still sharper goad to make haste and reveal the heavenly secrets shown her."[2] A lengthy illness, which Hildegard attributed to her refusal to follow the will of God, warned her not to delay writing down her visions any longer: "In this vision I was forced under heavy pains to reveal what I had seen and heard." Finally, she entrusted herself to her teacher, Volmar, because, as she writes, nothing was further from his thoughts than "the curious kind of many people's questioning." Therefore,

he listened generously to these strange tales. He marvelled at them, and ordered me to discreetly write them out until he could see what they were and where they came from. But as soon as he concluded

that they were from God, he made them known to his Abbot, and
from then on was very keen to work with me in these things.[3]

The events that were to follow, in which only clergy and
monks—spiritual men—were able to examine and pass judgment on the visionary experience of this virgin, seem to be an
arbitrary process. This makes it understandable why Hildegard feared and was ashamed to talk about her experiences
for decades. Her *Vita* reports in detail that Abbot Kuno at
first "was perplexed for his part at the strangeness and the
novelty of the matter," and then "was also aware that nothing
is impossible to God." Then he called "the wisest men of the
monastery and let them judge about what he had heard. He
questioned Hildegard about her writings and visions, and
advised her to proclaim what had come down from God to
her." But "not content with his own favourable judgement,
[he] saw to it that the matter should be brought to public no-
tice. He went to Mainz, the metropolitan See, and before the
venerable Archbishop Henry and the cathedral chapter, made
known what he had learned and showed them the writings
which the blessed virgin had lately produced."[4]

Hildegard was clever enough not to leave the judgment
on her visionary gift only to these clerics. In 1147, she took
the initiative to write a letter to Bernard of Clairvaux, and in
doing so, showed her extraordinary sense of the realities in the
church and the world. In fact, Bernard was probably the most
influential man of her time. To him Hildegard humbly calls
herself *"una paupercula feminea forma,"* a "poor little female"
in the sense of "pitiful in her being as a woman":

O venerable father Bernard, . . . I beseech you in the name of
the Living God to give heed to my queries. Father, I am greatly
disturbed by a vision which has appeared to me through divine
revelation, a vision seen not with my fleshly eyes but only in my

spirit. Wretched, and indeed more than wretched in my womanly condition, I have from earliest childhood seen great marvels which my tongue has no power to express but which the Spirit of God has taught me that I may believe.[5]

After two letters from her, Bernard gave an answer in which he endorses Hildegard's visionary gift as grace, and at the same time he admonishes her:

Brother Bernard, called Abbot of Clairvaux, offers to Hildegard, beloved daughter in Christ, whatever the prayer of a sinner can accomplish. . . . We rejoice in the grace of God which is in you. And, further, we most earnestly urge and beseech you to recognize this gift as grace and to respond eagerly to it with all humility and devotion, with the knowledge that "God resisteth the proud, and giveth grace to the humble" [James 4:6; 1 Pet 5:5].[6]

This letter of confirmation would turn into Hildegard's best strategic step because when Pope Eugene III, a Cistercian and disciple of Bernard, presided over the synod in Trier in 1147–1148, Archbishop Henry brought the matter of Hildegard's visions to his attention.

The prelate of Mainz and his senior clergy thereupon decided that they should journey to Trier and seek an apostolic judgment so that it could be ascertained by his authority what ought to be upheld and what rejected. Now the Pope, who was possessed of great discretion, was astonished to hear of such a novelty. But since he too knew that all things are possible to God (cf. Lk. 1:37, 18:27) he was keen to investigate the matter more thoroughly. So he sent the venerable Bishop of Verdun, Albero and with him his secretary Adalbert, and other suitable persons, to the monastery where Hildegard had lived enclosed these many years. They were to find out from her own person what it was about without any commotion or intrusive curiosity. So they put her at her ease as they made their enquiries, and she revealed without fear the facts concerning herself. They then returned to the Pope and reported

what they had heard to him and all of his attendants, who had
been waiting most expectantly. Once the Pope had accepted the
report, he gave orders that the blessed Hildegard's writings be
presented publicly, for they had been brought from the monastery
above mentioned and given to him. Holding them in his own hands
and himself taking the part of reader, he publicly read them out
to the Archbishop, the Cardinals and all of the clergy present.[7]

The council was unanimously impressed, especially since
Bernard chose this moment to intercede for the visionary who
had sought his aid. Following his suggestion, Pope Eugene
sent a letter to Hildegard:

[He] visited the blessed virgin with a letter of greeting in which
under Christ and in the name of blessed Peter, he granted her
permission to make known whatever she learnt through the Holy
Spirit and encouraged her to put it into writing.[8]

From this point on, Hildegard's fame grew steadily until
her death, as did the circle of her correspondents.

However, there was one "mistake" that she did not make
again. From then on, she no longer wrote as a weak woman in
her own name, but instead she spoke as a prophet and a seer of
the Living Light in the name of God. And she announced that
in that effeminate time in which the learned male clerics had
become lax, weak and fragile—in other words, effeminate—
and did not obey, that just in this "*muliebre tempus*" God had
paradoxically entrusted his mission to a woman, to shame
them by his words from her mouth and to strengthen them,
just as it is written:

But God chose what is foolish in the world to shame the wise;
God chose what is weak in the world to shame the strong; God
chose what is low and despised in the world, things that are not,
to reduce to nothing things that are, so that no one might boast in
the presence of God. (1 Cor 1:27-29)

It is precisely this conviction that underlay Hildegard's own prophetic call as she expressed it at the beginning of *Scivias*:

> *O fragile human, ashes of ashes, and filth of filth! Say and write what you see and hear. But since you are timid in speaking, and simple in expounding, and untaught in writing, speak and write these things not by a human mouth, and not by the understanding of human invention, and not by the requirements of human composition, but as you see and hear them on high in the heavenly places in the wonders of God. Explain these things in such a way that the hearer, recalling the words of his instructor, may expound them in those words, according to that will, vision and instruction. Thus therefore, O human, speak these things that you see and hear. And write them not by yourself or any other human being, but by the will of Him Who knows, sees and disposes all things in the secrets of His mysteries.*[9]

STAGE 7

Braunweiler – Dalberg with Dalburg Castle – Spabrücken – "Path of the Three Madonnas" – Schöneberg – Stromberg

7

Braunweiler – Dalberg with Dalburg Castle – Spabrücken – "Path of the Three Madonnas" – Schöneberg – Stromberg

Length 19.5 km – ca. 4.5 hrs. – Ascent 412 m – Descent 462 m – medium

Today's seventh stage is in its length and its contents something for "real" pilgrims. The morning begins at the St. Joseph Catholic Church in Braunweiler; there is a meditation tableau on "The Jealousy of God" (**Tableau 44**). Passing the Braunweiler fields and forest (*Hegewald*), the Hildegard Way leads about four kilometers upwards to Dalberg. The wayside crosses already show us that we are moving culturally so to speak from

Pilgrimage group at a cross outside of Braunweiler

the rather Protestant Western Naheland more deeply into the Catholic Soonwald.

At the edge of the forest, Keber's Cross stands at the beginning of the traditional pilgrimage that leads afoot to the old pilgrimage site of Spabrücken.

The tableau "Hildegard's Marian Songs" (**Tableau 45**) represents the special topic of this stage, namely, Mary, who is worshipped by Catholics as the "Mother of God." A Marian column (*Mariensäule*) at the foot of Dalburg Castle is dedicated to her. The sculpture showing the symbolism of moon and serpent was situated here on the old pilgrimage route to the "Madonna of Soon." For the

At the ruins of Dalburg castle (right, top);
Spabrücken Cloister Church (right, bottom)

faithful of many generations this has been a site of rest and of praying the "Hail Mary" on the way to the Mother of God of the Soon Forest (*Gottesmutter vom Soon*).

The next meditation tableau is at St. Leonard's Chapel in Dalberg (**Tableau 46**, "The Stone Wall of the Old Law").

Above, at the ruin site of Dalburg Castle, still owned by the Prince of Salm-Salm, there is also a chapel and another meditation tableau (**Tableau 47**, "The Pillar of the Trinity").

Finally, a 1.8-kilometer path leads to the old pilgrimage site of Spabrücken and the famous "Black Madonna of the Soon." There, the history of pilgrimage is told on **Tableau 48**. The "*Mariä Himmelfahrt*" (Mary's Assumption) cloister church was built by the Franciscans in the spirit of the Counter-Reformation (1721–1732). Yet, long before the Franciscans came here, there was a pilgrimage to Spabrücken (the name means "bridge crossing the Spach creek"). The first mention of it goes back to the year 1338. The miraculous wooden sculpture (*Gnadenbild*) is ninety centimeters high and probably dates from the mid-fourteenth century. Those who want to join the traditional pilgrimage should come here on Mary's feast day on September 8, or

join the candlelight procession on the evening before, that is, September 7 every year.

At the church, there is another meditation tableau for the Hildegard Way (**Tableau 49**, "The Pillar of the Savior's Humanity").

Next, the Hildegard Way follows the "Path of the Three Madonnas" (*Drei-Madonnen-Weg*) that was designed only recently by local people. They connected the starting point at the Black Madonna

"Black Madonna of the Soon" dressed on her Fiest Day

in Spabrücken with the topic "Faith." All Hildegard pilgrims are also invited to reflect on Mary while on this path.

The second stage of the "Path of the Three Madonnas" is the so-called *"Eremitage"* together with the wooden "Stations of the Cross." It is to be found in the middle of the forest on the way to Schöneberg. This second Madonna is connected with the topic of "Love."

At the *Eremitage* (where the Madonna-figure actually is missing), there is also a meditation tableau (**Tableau 50**, "The Tower of the Church").

The Way to Schöneberg then leads across open land, and thus we already can see the neo-Romanesque church from afar. This Catholic Church of the Finding of the Cross (*Kreuzauffindung*) actually contains a real surprise, namely, a post-war photocopy of the so-called "Madonna of Stalingrad." The circumstances under which this image came into the parish church of Schöneberg and is now, as the third Madonna on the way, connected with the topic of "Hope" have a special story which is reported on a tableau in the church:

> *"Madonna of Stalingrad." This name was given to her by the German soldiers in the fateful Christmas days of 1942. The image was created in a German bunker on the back side of a Russian map. The German senior physician Dr. Kurt Reuter from Wichmannshausen near Eschwege in Hessia drew it for his men; it was a Christmas present for the enclosed, hopeless troops. The image was saved; the*

On the pilgrimage route from Dalberg to Spabrücken

Schöneberg Church with "Hildegarden" in front (above, left); copy of *The Madonna of Stalingrad* in the church (above, right)

one who created it died in 1944 as a Russian prisoner of war. After the war, the Schöneberg priest, Pastor Felix Groß, a friend of the Reuter family and also a former minister in Stalingrad, who had been seriously wounded and evacuated, acquired a photocopy of this drawing. And that is how the Madonna of Stalingrad came to the parish church of Schöneberg.

At the church of Schöneberg, there is also a meditation tableau (**Tableau 51**, "The Son of Man").

The way from Schöneberg then leads through the forest to the vacation village of Schindeldorf. There we find a tableau about Hildegard's book on virtues and vices (**Tableau 52**, "*Liber Vitae Meritorum*").

From Schindeldorf, the way through the forest to Stromberg is not far off.

Vaults in the church of Schöneberg

O quam pretiosa

O quam pretiosa est	O how precious
virginitas Virginis huius,	is the virginity of this virgin!
quae clausam portam habet,	Her portal is closed,
et cuius viscera sancta	and her womb the holy
Divinitas	Godhead
calore suo infudit,	flooded with this warmth,
ita quod flos in ea crevit,	so a flower grew within her.
et Filius Dei	And the Son of God came
	forth
per secreta ipsius	from her secret chamber
quasi aurora exivit.	like the dawn.
Unde dulce germen,	Thus the tender shoot
quod ipsius Filius est,	that is her Son
per clausuram ventris eius	opened paradise
paradisum aperuit.	through the cloister of her
	womb.
Et Filius Dei	And the Son of God came
	forth
per secreta ipsius	from her secret chamber
quasi aurora exivit.	like the dawn.

Hildegard of Bingen[1]

TABLEAU 44

The Zeal of God

St. Josef Church, Braunweiler

Liber Scivias III.5

PILGRIM'S REFLECTION

What would it be like if justice would prevail in this world?

Who should make that happen?

With all the evil, horrible and unjust events in the world, have I ever wished that there should be some kind of final justice?

_____

_____

_____

_____

_____

_____

_____

_____

_____

_____

"After this, I looked, and behold! In the north corner . . . there appeared a head of marvelous form. . . . It had three wings of wondrous breadth and length."

In this fifth vision of the third book of *Scivias*, Hildegard envisions the enraged, fiery red head of God looking towards the North; this is the direction from which the devil and his demons threaten humankind. His three powerfully flapping wings represent the expansion of the power of the threefold God and ensure that the justice of God takes place in all directions. Thus, the figure of the "Zeal of God" does not show false complacency in the face of evildoing; rather, it measures and judges good and evil as though by "consuming fire, windstorm, double-edged sword, lightning, thunder."

Moses and the Ten Commandments
Picture detail from *Liber Scivias* I.5

I am the LORD your God, who brought you out of the land of Egypt, out of the house of slavery; you shall have no other gods before me.

You shall not make for yourself an idol, whether in the form of anything that is in heaven above, or that is on the earth beneath, or that is in the water under the earth. You shall not bow down to them or worship them; for I the LORD your God am a jealous God, punishing children for the iniquity of parents, to the third and the fourth generation of those who reject me, but showing steadfast love to the thousandth generation of those who love me and keep my commandments.

You shall not make wrongful use of the name of the LORD your God, for the LORD will not acquit anyone who misuses his name.

Remember the sabbath day, and keep it holy. Six days you shall labor and do all your work. But the seventh day is a sabbath to the LORD your God; you shall not do any work—you, your son or your daughter, your male or female slave, your livestock, or the alien resident in your towns. For in six days the LORD made heaven and earth, the sea, and all that is in them, but rested the seventh day; therefore the LORD blessed the sabbath day and consecrated it.

Honor your father and your mother, so that your days may be long in the land that the LORD your God is giving you.

You shall not murder.

You shall not commit adultery.

You shall not steal.

You shall not bear false witness against your neighbor.

You shall not covet your neighbor's house; you shall not covet your neighbor's wife, or male or female slave, or ox, or donkey, or anything that belongs to your neighbor.

Exodus 20:2-17

TABLEAU 45

Hildegard's Marian Songs

Site of Keber's Cross

"Mary," picture detail from *Liber Scivias* III.13

"Priceless integrity! Her virgin gate opened to none. But the Holy One flooded her with warmth until a flower sprang in her womb and the Son of God came forth from the secret chamber like the dawn."

Twenty-one songs out of the seventy-seven gathered in Hildegard's *Symphonia harmoniae caelestium revelationum* are dedicated to Mary, the mother of Jesus. In the Dendermonde manuscript, supervised by the author, those songs take an important place just after those dedicated to God.

According to Hildegard, Mary is the link between paradise and the world after the Fall in which we are now living. The incarnation of God in the Virgin is seen as the main act of salvation that was already in the mind of God before the beginning of time.

Mary has all virtues—humility above all—and she redeems the negative vision of the feminine condition (*feminea forma*) that, after her, shines as a mirror of divine creation. To express the updated perennial meaning of that chapter of salvation, to which Mary is the key, Hildegard uses a wide number of metaphors and poetic expressions of great strength and beauty that symbolically describe a higher reality.

She often uses words and phrases related to nature such as evergreen branch, splendid gem, lucid or golden material, dawn or star of the sea. She also describes incarnation as the warmest, brightest, most musical and most joyful expression of divine love, embodied in Mary.

Margarida Barbal Rodoreda

**Annette Esser, *Annunciation*,
gold leaf and oil on canvas, 60 x 70 cm, 2016**

TABLEAU 46

The Stone Wall of the Old Law

St. Leonhard Chapel in Dalberg

Liber Scivias III.6

PILGRIM'S REFLECTION

What perception and what opinion do I have about the church?

What attitudes and qualities should leaders and co-workers in the church or in other important institutions have?

_____

_____

_____

_____

_____

_____

_____

_____

_____

_____

_____

_____

"And after this, I saw the wall of the aforementioned building which ran between the north and west corners. . . . And inside the building I saw six figures."

In the sixth vision of the third book, the *Liber Scivias*, Hildegard envisions the stone wall of the City of God, which consists of three consecutive walls. In the arcades of the first wall are the spiritual guides, then the other orders follow hierarchically. On the outside, the threefold wall provides protection. On the inside, it is inhabited by wonderfully acting figures, namely, the virtues, whose attitudes represent the construction of the City of God in the best sense: (1) Abstinence, (2) Liberality, (3) Piety, (4) Truth, (5) Peace, (6) Beatitude. Two more figures are sitting on the wall: (1) Discretion, (2) Salvation of the Souls.

I was glad when they said to me, / "Let us go to the house of the LORD!" / Our feet are standing / within your gates, O Jerusalem. / Jerusalem—built as a city / that is bound firmly together. / To it the tribes go up, / the tribes of the LORD, / as was decreed for Israel, / to give thanks to the name of the LORD. / For there the thrones for judgment were set up, / the thrones of the house of David. / Pray for the peace of Jerusalem: / "May they prosper who love you. / Peace be within your walls, / and security within your towers." / For the sake of my relatives and friends / I will say, "Peace be within you." / For the sake of the house of the LORD our God, / I will seek your good.

Psalm 122

Reflection

Bottling everything up
belittling oneself
feeling guilty for everything
apologizing unasked immediately
demoralizing oneself inwardly
always cursing
is sin.

Speaking out about things
accepting compliments
showing oneself responsible
considering one's own failure carefully
building up inwardly
praying to God
is grace

Annette Esser

TABLEAU 47

The Pillar of the Trinity

Dalberg Castle Ruin Site

Liber Scivias III.7

PILGRIM'S REFLECTION

What is belief, what is disbelief,
and what is wrong belief for me?

THE PILLAR OF THE TRINITY

"Then I saw in the west corner of the building a wondrous, secret and supremely strong pillar, purple-black in color. . . . The outside part had three steel-colored edges, which stood out like sharp sword-edges from the bottom to the top."

In this seventh vision of the third book of *Scivias*, Hildegard envisions God's Trinity again. But this time it is not about the inner life of the Trinity (as in *Scivias* II.4) but rather about its outward agency. In this regard, the pillar of Christian teaching shows its "sharp edges" towards three sides: (1) the stiff straw symbolizes the falling away from "true faith"; (2) the disheveled feathers symbolize religious presumptuousness; (3) and the cropped, rotten woods signify illusions or heresies. Thus, "This Pillar of the Trinity" is administering judgment in the West, the direction of the sunset, the coming darkness and closeness to death.

Then the LORD said to me, "You have seen well, for I am watching over my word to perform it." . . .

And I will utter my judgments against them, for all their wickedness in forsaking me. . . . But you, gird up your loins; stand up and tell them everything that I command you. Do not break down before them, or I will break you before them. And I for my part have made you today a fortified city, an iron pillar, and a bronze wall, against the whole land. . . . They will fight against you; but they shall not prevail against you, for I am with you, says the LORD, to deliver you.

Jeremiah 1:12, 16-19

TABLEAU 48

Pilgrimage

Spabrücken

Spabrücken is an old pilgrimage site. It existed long before the Franciscans came in the seventeenth century and founded their church in the spirit of the Counter-Reformation. Its origins are unknown, but in the center stands a Marian statue from the fourteenth century that drew pilgrims who came from the Rhine or from Saarbrücken via Kirn into the Soonwald. And even today, September 8, the feast of Mary's birth, remains the main pilgrimage day in Spabrücken.

The history of pilgrimage is old. At all times and in different religions, people set out for places where they believed they could be closer to God or gods and goddesses or at least make contact with divine powers. In the Christian world, the word "pilgrim" derives from *peregrinus*, a person who goes abroad. Since the fourth century, the faithful searched for the path to Jerusalem in order to walk in the footsteps of Christ. Later on, the pilgrimage to Rome began. And, already in the ninth century, the pilgrimage to the grave of the apostle James in Santiago de Compostela played an important role. In Hildegard's lifetime, these three constituted the *peregrinatio maior*, the great pilgrimage.

Also, Jutta of Sponheim (1092–1136) wanted to undertake a pilgrimage into the Holy Land to Jerusalem, from which the Crusaders had reported much (First Crusade of 1096). But she was hindered by her brother, Earl Meinhard of Sponheim, and instead became a nun at the Disibodenberg monastery.

> *After her mother was taken from their midst, Jutta made arrangements so she would not have to delay in carrying out her plan, that is, to leave her native land and her father's house (cf. Gen. 12:1) for the Lord. The Lord however arranged things for her in another way. For when her brother Meinhard became aware of it, he considered that, as far as he was concerned, her departure was not to be tolerated. He worked to head off his sister's pilgrimage. (The Life of Lady Jutta, Recluse)[2]*

Michael Vesper

223

TABLEAU 49

The Pillar of the Savior's Humanity

Spabrücken Pilgrimage Church

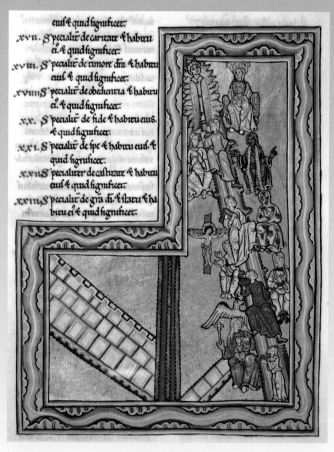

Liber Scivias III.8

PILGRIM'S REFLECTION

How does God come to humankind?

How do we as human beings find our way to God?

THE PILLAR OF THE SAVIOR'S HUMANITY

"And then I saw, on the south side of the wall . . . a great and shadowed pillar, which protruded both inside and outside the building."

In the eighth vision of the third book of *Scivias*, the virtues on the "Pillar of the Savior's Humanity" climb down from heaven and up from earth just as the angels do on Jacob's ladder (Gen 28:10-14). In this vision, Hildegard unfolds her central thought that God's incarnation also initiated and made possible the co-operation between God and humankind to build up the City of God. This is because the divine virtues also descended together with the Son of God, and, through his divinity, humans who work with these virtues will find their way to God. At the top of the pillar stands God's mercy in the form a bishop. From here downwards are seven female figures: on the right side, Humility, Love, Fear of God, and Obedience; and, on the left side, Faith, Hope, and Chastity.

Jacob left Beer-sheba and went toward Haran. He came to a certain place and stayed there for the night, because the sun had set. Taking one of the stones of the place, he put it under his head and lay down in that place. And he dreamed that there was a ladder set up on the earth, the top of it reaching to heaven; and the angels of God were ascending and descending on it. And the LORD stood beside him and said, "I am the LORD, the God of Abraham your father and the God of Isaac; the land on which you lie I will give to you and to your offspring; and your offspring shall be like the dust of the earth, and you shall spread abroad to the west and to the east and to the north and to the south; and all the families of the earth shall be blessed in you and in your offspring. Know that I am with you and will keep you wherever you go, and will bring you back to this land; for I will not leave you until I have done what I have promised you." Then Jacob woke from his sleep and said, "Surely the LORD is in this place—and I did not know it!"

Genesis 28:10-16

SONG

O viridissima virga

O Greenest Branch

Never was leaf so green,
for you branched from the spirited
blast of the quest of the saints.

When it came time
for your boughs to blossom
(I salute you!)
your scent was like balsam
distilled in the sun.

And your flower made all spices
fragrant
dry though they were:
they burst into verdure.

So the skies rained dew on the grass
and the whole earth exulted,
for her womb brought forth wheat,
for the birds of heaven
made their nests in it.

Keepers of the feast, rejoice!
The banquet's ready. And you
sweet maid-child
are a fount of gladness.

But Eve?
She despised every joy.
Praise nonetheless,
praise to the Highest.

Hildegard of Bingen[3]

TABLEAU 50

The Tower of the Church

Eremitage

Liber Scivias III.9

When I see the church as crooked,
how can I help to rectify it?

In my life, do I listen to the voice of wisdom?

THE TOWER OF THE CHURCH

"And this I saw, in front of the pillar of the humanity of the Savior, a tower of brilliant splendor."

In this ninth vision of the third book of *Scivias*, Hildegard envisions the "Tower of the Church." Work on this crooked tower has not yet ended but it is already crowned with seven battlements that represent the seven gifts of the Holy Spirit: Wisdom, Reason, Counsel, Strength, Knowledge, Piety, and Fear of God. Within the tower of the church, the baptized ones climb up as though on a ladder (cf. *Scivias* III.8). Some apostles, saints or teachers of the church already beam from above with clarity.

In front of the tower of the church, there is a temple with seven pillars (cf. Prov 9:1). On it is Lady Wisdom, who calls to human beings to come to her. At her left side, the huge figure of Justice stands (with a banner), and to her right stands Fortitude (as a knight with a sword); to the far right is the figure

of Sanctity, which has two more facets: the face of joy to the right and the face of self-sacrifice to the left.

Pillar in Sponheim Minster

SONG

Sonne der Gerechtigkeit—Sun of Justice

Sonne der Gerechtigkeit—Sun of Justice
gehe auf zu unsrer Zeit—rise in our time
brich in deiner Kirche an—rise in your church
dass die Welt es sehen kann—that the world can see it
Erbarm' dich Herr—Be merciful, o Lord!

Weck' die tote Christenheit—Wake up dead Christianity
aus dem Schlaf der Sicherheit—from its sleep of security
dass sie deine Stimme hört—that it listen to your voice
sich zu deinem Wort bekehrt—that it convert to your word
Erbarm' dich Herr—Be merciful, o Lord!

Gib den Boten Kraft und Mut—Give power and courage to
the messengers
Glauben, Hoffnung, Liebesglut—Faith, hope and fire of love
und lass reiche Frucht aufgehn—and let rich fruit arise
Wo sie unter Tränen sä'n—where they sow while in tears
Erbarm' dich Herr—Be merciful, o Lord!

German Church Hymn[4]

TABLEAU 51

The Son of Man

Church in Schöneberg

Liber Scivias III.10

PILGRIM'S REFLECTION

What moral values do I regard as most important
in my life?

What virtues are decisive on my way to God?

"And after this, I saw on the summit of the eastern corner of the building . . . seven white marble steps, which rose like an arch up to the great stone on which the shining One sat on the throne."

In this tenth vision of the third book of *Scivias*, Hildegard envisions the Son of God as he looks down from his throne to humankind: "O foolish people! You languidly and shamefully shrink into yourselves, and do not want to open an eye to see how good your souls could be." In front of him stand the five most important of the thirty-five virtues. These are the figures of Constancy, in whose breast is the thirsting deer (cf. Ps 42:2); the golden figure of Desire for Heaven at her right side and the green figure of Compunction. Below her, with the wheel of perfection, is the figure of Contempt for the World, and the figure with angelic wings below is Concord envisioning peace.

"When the Son of Man comes in his glory, and all the angels with him, then he will sit on the throne of his glory. All the nations will be gathered before him, and he will separate people one from another as a shepherd separates the sheep from the goats, and he will put the sheep at his right hand and the goats at the left. Then the king will say to those at his right hand, 'Come, you that are blessed by my Father, inherit the kingdom prepared for you from the foundation of the world; for I was hungry and you gave me food, I was thirsty and you gave me something to drink, I was a stranger and you welcomed me, I was naked and you gave me clothing, I was sick and you took care of me, I was in prison and you visited me.' Then the righteous will answer him, 'Lord, when was it that we saw you hungry and gave you food, or thirsty and gave you something to drink? And when was it that we saw you a stranger and welcomed you, or naked and gave you clothing? And when was it that we saw you sick or in prison and visited you?' And the king will answer them, 'Truly I tell you, just as you did it to one of the least of these who are members of my family, you did it to me.' Then he will say to those at his left hand, 'You that are accursed, depart from me into the eternal fire prepared for the devil and his angels; for I was hungry and you gave me no food, I was thirsty and you gave me nothing to drink, I was a stranger and you did not welcome me, naked and you did not give me clothing, sick and in prison and you did not visit me.' Then they also will answer, 'Lord, when was it that we saw you hungry or thirsty or a stranger or naked or sick or in prison, and did not take care of you?' Then he will answer them, 'Truly I tell you, just as you did not do it to one of the least of these, you did not do it to me.' And these will go away into eternal punishment, but the righteous into eternal life."

Matthew 25:31-46

Praying for Divine Virtues

God, Alpha and Omega of the cosmos.
Beginning and end of our life.
Origin of the world and judge at the end of time.

Let us realize that our own life has meaning,
That it does matter which path we walk in our lives,
That we can decide which direction we take.
We can choose to become a living human being who accomplishes something in this world,
Or a lifeless creature who surrenders to addictions, to sex and consumerism.

Let us perceive that our soul is endangered and this choice is not easy,
That we ourselves are torn this way and that between virtues and vices,
That in striving to do what is right and just we might become enmeshed in wrongs again,
That we are always in need of your mercy and power.
In your mercy you have let your son *Jesus Christ* become human.
If we direct our lives to him, we will understand what love and justice is.

As Christians we confess that your son sits on the "throne" on your right from where he will come at the "Last Judgment" at the end of time to judge the living and the dead. However we might imagine this, you have given your son to us as the measure and the orientation of our life. We know that in the end we will be judged according to what we have done or not done to the least of our brothers and sisters. But we will not be judged because Christ wants to condemn us. Rather, it will be what we have done in the spirit of love, and also what we have failed to do, carelessly and without love, that will judge us: spiritually upright or humanly cast down.

Yet, according to Saint Hildegard, you have also given us five divine virtues at our side, so that we might walk in the upright way: constancy (*constancia*); desire for heaven (*desiderium caelestis*); compunction (*compunctio*); contempt of the world (*contemptio mundi*); and concordance (*concordia*).

Constancy is like a pillar that builds up our body when we meditate and rest deeply in ourselves. Then we find security within ourselves. But this security might also render us numb and degenerate into seeking materialistic safety.

Therefore what grows out of a well-grounded constancy is *the desire for heavenly joy*. Like a deer our soul thirsts for the fullness of life. Yet it is precisely when we have found the greatest happiness that we might become complacent and fall.

Therefore it is good that remorse overcomes us as soon as we start to become arrogant about our own luck, or if we even start to think that we have deserved something better than others. Yes, even *compunction*, the sad look into the darkness and the abysses of our own soul, into the moments in which we have failed, or had evil thoughts, or acted egoistically, is a divine virtue. It is in fact an act of humility. For it means no less than perceiving ourselves and our own truth in the light of God's truth, love, and justice. For God's own self is the truth in whose mirror we may recognize our own imperfections, faults, and weaknesses.

But even if we want to follow Christ humbly and perfectly, if we want to be perfectly just and perfectly loving, we will fail. The more we long to follow this path, the greater will be the abysses that open up and the farther we will seem to be from our ideals, until we finally understand that the path of perfection is not straight. Rather the path of truth attracts us to the green meadow where, besides beautiful flowers and strong branches, we also experience natural unevenesses and threats from nature itself. The path of the green power of life, this path in which we engage in life, this path in which our community (of the church) might also receive "wounds and bruises," can practically never be straight. Still, this path can become "round." It can become enclosed in a perfect circle. This is when we recognize that it is not ourselves who can achieve this but only you, O God, who can make us perfect.

If, by your virtue, we succeed in *disengaging* ourselves from the temptations of consumerism and the unbearable lightness of being, then you will finally make our life perfect. Entering into a new circle of *concordance* with your will, we will finally find peace. Then it will be as if we stand in the midst of the choirs of angels and join in unison with them in a song of love and justice. This is bliss. Then we are blessed with bliss. Then we have found our way to the choir of the blessed ones. Hallelujah.

God our Father and our Mother, you love us and you know us. Let us discern your mercy and virtues in our lives, so that we can walk in your path with power. Amen.

To the Vision "The Son of Man" by Hildegard of Bingen
in *Liber Scivias III.10*

Annette Esser

TABLEAU 52

Liber Vitae Meritorum

Schindeldorf

"The Fountain of Life," *Liber Divinorum Operum* III.3

Liber Vitae Meritorum is Hildegard's second theological work. It describes the fight between the destructive and constructive powers in human beings. Hildegard names them vices and virtues. They are ordered dramaturgically in thirty-five contradictory pairs. A vice always speaks first, and is then contradicted by a virtue.

At first, the vices seem quite reasonable:

"Why should I exert and stress myself out because of somebody else?" (*Hard-heartedness*)

"Why should I be hungry and thirsty?" (*Gluttony*)

"Who at all could say everything truthfully?" (*Falseness*)

Yet, the answers of the virtues reveal the destructive and hostile power of the vices:

"Oh, you of stone, what are you saying? . . . I am an ointment for each pain and my words are right." (*Mercy* against *Hard-heartedness*)

"Nobody plucks a harp in such a way that its strings break." (*Abstinence*)

"Oh, your tongue is from a serpent." (*Truth*)

Thus, the virtues as divine powers do not at all formulate a moral appeal to which the readers should subject themselves; rather they demonstrate how the apparent advantage of the vice results in personal damage instead.

For instance, if someone ignores others and in his hard-heartedness builds a wall around himself, he finds himself in solitude and isolation. Community, sympathy and meaningful goals, as well as hope beyond this life, belong to a fulfilled and content life. Healing measures for this are insight and willingness to change.

Michael Ptok

STAGE 8

Stromberg –
Warmsroth –
Ruheforst –
"Jägerhaus" –
Morgenbachtal –
Rhein-Burgen-Weg –
Bingerbrück

8

Stromberg – Warmsroth – Ruheforst – "Jägerhaus" – Morgenbachtal – Rhein-Burgen-Weg – Bingerbrück

Length 19.6 km – 5.5 hrs. – Ascent 386 m – Descent 527 m – medium

The eighth stage is the last big hiking stage on the Hildegard Way and leads us through the beautiful landscapes of the Soonwald trail (*Soonwaldsteig*), Bingen Forest and the Rhine Castles Trail (*Rhein-Burgen-Weg*), with a view of Bingen on the Rhine.

The morning starts at St. Jakobus Church in Stromberg; the church name itself signifies that here we are already on the Camino de Santiago. The meditation tableau "The Last Days and the Fall of the Antichrist" (**Tableau 53**) is placed promi-

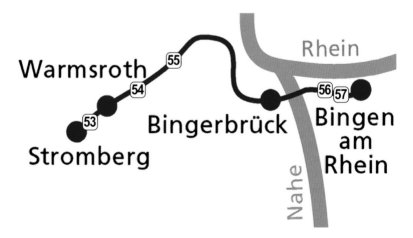

In the Morgenbachtal

nently in front of the church. It relates to yesterday's tableau and gives us the theme of the day: Hildegard's apocalyptic visions, which for a long time were the sole basis for her fame.

The way from Stromberg leads us to nearby Warmsroth and the St. Pankratius Chapel in Wald-Erbach. At this newly restored chapel, the foundation of which was laid in the fifteenth century and present shape is from 1716, we find the next meditation tableau (**Tableau 54**, "The Last Judgment, the New Heaven and the New Earth").

Behind a manor house and garden, the Hildegard Way turns sharply to the left into the Waldalgesheim forest.

At the end of the forest burial site "Ruheforst," we find the last meditation tableau on the Hildegard Way. Its topic, "Symphony of Praise," invites us to rest, listen to music or even sing, and maybe also reflect upon the so-called "last things" (**Tableau 55**, Music: "*O gloriosissimi lux*").

From this point on there is a beautiful walking path to Bingerbrück. It takes us first through the "Steckeschlääferk-

Troll figure carved into a tree in the "Steckeschlääferklamm" (right, top); at St. Pankratius Church in Wald-Erbach (right, bottom)

245

View to the Rhine River near Bingen

lamm." Here, carved faces popping up in trees give a feeling of being in a fairy-tale forest.

Halfway through today's eighth stage, the pilgrim has earned a rest. We are invited to stay in the "Jägerhaus," where mostly meat dishes but also vegetarian meals are on the menu.

The way from there leads us through Bingen Forest down through the Morgenbachtal, a valley with a small brook.

At the new forester's house, "Heiligkreuz" signs let us know how the Hildegard Way converges here with the Camino de Santiago and the Rhine Castles Trail. From there, it is not far to a first viewpoint of the Rhine valley near Assmannshausen.

Walking on the Rhine Castle Trail, with its view of the Middle Rhine Valley (since 2002 UNESCO World Heritage Site) is also a great joy for all friends of Hildegard.

At the lookout point "Prinzen-kopf," there is a view of the Rhine Valley, with Bingen to the right (west) and Rüdesheim to the left (east) and the Bingen Mouse Tower (*Mäuseturm*) directly ahead.

From there, it is not far to Bingen, where Hildegard moved to in 1150 in order to found her first abbey at the Rupertsberg.

Bench in the Bingen Forest

The Great Woman Mystic

Writer of great theological
works
Founder of monasteries
Traveler with a mission
Preacher of the word of God
Hildegard was powerless
In a man's world
But she rose to power
Through the will of God
"Thy will be done"
Fiat voluntas tua
She maintained
The fear of God
Timor Dei
She overcame
Poverty in spirit
Paupertas
She gifted us with
A prophetic ministry
She maintained her humble-
ness towards God
While she stood her ground
Towards humankind.

She became
A great woman mystic
She gives us puzzles
To solve
She gives us questions
To answer
She gives us messages
Which are difficult to
understand
She gives us hope
She reveals secrets of the
Holy Scripture
That we have trouble
comprehending
She gives us clues
She teaches us mysteries
She tries to help us
To find
Our way to God
And salvation.

Karen S. E. Stock

TABLEAU 53

The Last Days and the Fall of the Antichrist

St. Jakobus Church, Stromberg

Liber Scivias III.11

How do I perceive the time in which we live today?

Can I imagine that injustice, evil, lies and violence symbolically "stink to heaven"?

Will this ever end?

_____

_____

_____

_____

_____

_____

_____

_____

_____

_____

_____

_____

_____

THE LAST DAYS AND THE FALL OF
THE ANTICHRIST

"And then I looked to the North, and behold! five beasts stood there."

This eleventh vision of the third book of *Scivias* has made Hildegard famous as an apocalyptic visionary. In it, she foretells to her contemporaries the Antichrist's ravages as well as the coming five dark ages in the form of five wild beasts: the ages of the fiery dog, the dark yellow lion, the pale horse, the black pig and the grey wolf. At the end of time, when the Son of Man appears on his throne in the East (top right), his bride Ecclesia also shows herself; her abdomen exhibits the traces of vices (black) and of suffering (red). Even worse, Antichrist, the son of Lucifer, lifts his abominable head from her genitals: "I want to uplift my power between her legs." He nearly succeeds. Only at the end of times, after all his excessive arts of seduction, will a great mass of excrement visible as a giant cloud above the heads of humans be smashed by God with a loud bang and changed into a stinking fog.

A great portent appeared in heaven: a woman clothed with the sun, with the moon under her feet, and on her head a crown of twelve stars. She was pregnant and was crying out in birth pangs, in the agony of giving birth.

Revelation 12:1-2

Towards the End of Times

Yes, we have had them, these five ages
. . . in which human beings raged like snappish dogs and destroyed so much in this world;
. . . in which pugnacious rulers incited useless and brutal wars like maddened lions;
. . . in which men and women surrendered to their addiction to sex, drugs and consumption like pale horses;
. . . in which a vast majority of mankind gave in to dirty thoughts and all kinds of messes like dark pigs, and in which those who should have kept things under control have fallen into depression about them;
. . . in which powerful potentates clawed their way to the top and then exploited other humans, animals and all of nature ruthlessly.

Yes, we have had them and we still do have them, these times.
After we have seen the ravages of Nero and Hitler and ISIS, we say: Yes, it does exist, this fathomless evil. We have looked into its eyes. And we wish to pray:

Merciful God,
God of love,
God of justice,
. . . let us remember you as the true God;
. . . let us work against the evildoing that spreads itself out in hu-mankind and this world;
. . . let us recognize the true martyrs of our time;
. . . let us never forget what your love means for each of us who all are enmeshed in guilt.

God be merciful to all of us.
Amen

Annette Esser

TABLEAU 54

The Last Judgment

St. Jakobus Church, Stromberg

Liber Scivias III.12

Have I ever imagined the end of the world?

What do I know about the Jewish, Christian and Muslim belief in the Apocalypse and the Last Judgment?

THE LAST JUDGMENT

"After this I looked, and behold, all the elements and crea-
tures were shaken by dire convulsions; fire and air and water
burst forth, and the earth was made to move, lightning and
thunder crashed and mountains and forests fell, and all that
was mortal expired. And all the elements were purified, and
whatever had been foul in them vanished and was no more
seen. And I heard a voice resounding in a great cry throughout
the world, saying: 'O ye children of men who are lying in the
earth, rise up and all!' And behold, all the human bones in
whatever place in the earth they lay were brought together
in one moment and covered with their flesh; and they all rose
up with limbs and bodies intact, each in his or her gender."

In this twelfth vision of the third book of *Scivias*, Hildegard
describes the Last Judgment that ends on Judgment Day. As
good and bad deeds are then revealed at once, Hildegard also
names this the Day of Great Revelation. After all the deafen-
ing noise, an extensive calm unfolds and a New Heaven and
a New Earth will begin.

The hand of the LORD came upon me, and he brought me out by the
Spirit of the LORD and set me down in the middle of a valley; it was
full of bones. He led me all around them; there were very many lying
in the valley, and they were very dry. He said to me, "Mortal, can these
bones live?" I answered, "O LORD GOD, you know." Then he said to me,
"Prophesy to these bones, and say to them, O dry bones, hear the word
of the LORD. Thus says the LORD GOD to these bones: I will cause breath
to enter you, and you shall live. I will lay sinews on you, and will cause
flesh to come upon you, and cover you with skin, and put breath in you,
and you shall live, and you shall know that I am the LORD."

Ezekiel 37:1-6

Then I saw a new heaven and a new earth; for the first heaven and the first earth had passed away, and the sea was no more. And I saw the holy city, the new Jerusalem, coming down out of heaven from God, prepared as a bride adorned for her husband. And I heard a loud voice from the throne saying,

> "See, the home of God is among mortals.
> He will dwell with them;
> they will be his peoples,
> and God himself will be with them;
> he will wipe away every tear from their eyes.
> Death will be no more;
> mourning and crying and pain will be no more,
> for the first things have passed away."

And the one who was seated on the throne said, "See, I am making all things new." Also he said, "Write this, for these words are trustworthy and true." Then he said to me, "It is done! I am the Alpha and the Omega, the beginning and the end."

Revelation 21:1-6

TABLEAU 55

Symphony of Praise

"Ruheforst" Burial Site, Waldalgesheim

Liber Scivias III.13

PILGRIM'S REFLECTION

What song would we like to sing together here?

Can I imagine that we as human beings sing together with the choirs of the blessed and the choirs of the angels in heaven?

"Then I saw the lucent sky, in which I heard different kinds of music, marvelously embodying all the meanings I had heard before."

In the last vision of *Scivias,* Hildegard hears celestial music. Her inner seeing is at the same time an inner hearing. In the visionary image, Mary, to whom Hildegard has dedicated most of her songs, is enthroned above. Below her, the angels are singing in praise. In the five medallions below there are: the patriarchs and prophets above to the left; the apostles above to the right; the martyrs below to the left; the confessors below to the right; and, the virgins in the middle. Hildegard has written their hymns, laments and antiphons in text and notes (*neumen*). With this music, which we human beings on earth can sing together with the blessed ones in heaven, Hildegard's *Scivias* ends.

SONG

De Angelis

O most glorious angels

O gloriosissimi, lux vivens, Angeli,	O most glorious angels, living light:
qui infra Divinitatem divinos oculos	beneath the Divinity you gaze on the eyes of God
cum mystica obscuritate	within the mystical darkness
omnis creaturae aspicitis	of all creation
in ardentibus desideriis,	in ardent desires,
unde numquam potestis satiari.	so you can never be satiated.

Hildegard of Bingen[1]

Epilogue

In principio omnes creature viruerunt.	In the beginning all creation was verdant,
in medio flores floruerunt;	flowers blossomed in the midst of it;
postea viriditas descendit.	later, greenness sank away.
Et istud vir preliator vidit et dixit:	And the champion (Christ) saw this and said:
Hoc scio, sed aureus numerus nondem est plenus.	"I know it, but the golden number is not yet full.
Tu ergo, paternum speculum aspice:	You then, behold me, mirror of your fatherhood:
In corpore meo fatigationem sustineo,	in my body I am suffering exhaustion,
parvuli etiam mei deficiunt.	even my children faint.
Nunc memor esto, quod plenitude	Now remember that the fullness
que in primo facta est	which was made in the beginning
arescere non debuit,	need not have grown dry,
et tunc in te habuisti	and that then you resolved
quod oculus tuus numquam cederet	that your eye would never fail
usque dum corpus meum videres plenum gemmarum.	until you saw my body full of jewels.
Nam me fatigat quod omnia membra mea in irrisionem vadunt.	For it wearies me that all my limbs are exposed to mockery:

Pater, vide, vulnera mea tibi　　Father, behold, I am showing
　ostendo.　　　　　　　　　　you my wounds."
Ergo nunc, omnes homines　　So now, all you people,
genua vestra ad patrem　　　Bend your knees to the
　vestrum flectite.　　　　　　Father,
ut vobis manum suum　　　That he may reach you with
　porrigat.　　　　　　　　his hand.

Hildegard of Bingen[2]

POEM

Co-operation

Each of us has bright sides and shadowy sides,
each of us has strengths and weaknesses,
each of us has sides that we like and sides that we do not like.

This is even true for ourselves.
For, neither do others like everything about us nor do we like
everything about ourselves.

But this is also true:
We are loveable,
We have talents.
We are worth being treasured by others as well as by ourselves.

What does that mean for our teamwork, for our co-operation?

We have three options:
We can either stress our own strengths and harp on others'
weaknesses.
Or, we can admire others and their talents and belittle
ourselves.

Or, we perceive in ourselves and in others as well, talents as
well as weaknesses and deficits.
And, in our co-operation, we use our strengths and talents
wisely in order to balance the weaknesses and deficits of others, and vice versa.

Others are present where we have weaknesses, deficits and
shortages and help us up.

Only in this way can something positive, something
constructive, something loveable arise.

Perhaps, this is what Hildegard of Bingen calls synergy,
the co-operation of humankind in building the City of God.

In a book for children, I found this image:
What is heaven and what is hell?
In hell, all are sitting around a kettle of delicious soup.
Everyone has a long spoon in their hand.
Yet, the spoon is so long that nobody can feed themselves.
So, everybody is starving in front of the full kettle.
And what about heaven?
In heaven, all are sitting around a kettle of delicious soup.
Everyone has a long spoon in their hand. Because the spoon is
so long that nobody can feed themselves, people feed each other.
So everyone is filled.

So what is good co-operation?
It is not about what kind of soup we have,
It is rather about how we manage to spoon our soup together!

Alleluia.

Annette Esser

Fifth Station in Hildegard's Life: The Foundation of the Rupertsberg Women's Monastery

by Annette Esser

After Hildegard had become famous, the monastery of St. Disibod began to attract so many female postulants that they could not be housed any longer. For this reason, but perhaps also because the common life of monks and nuns in the monastery had become more difficult,[3] Hildegard thought about moving out:

> I saw in a vision and I was taught and compelled to make known to my superiors, that our place with all that belonged to it, should be separated from that place where I had been offered to God (the monastery Disibodenberg).[4]

The place where she now intended to found her own women's cloister was also shown to her by the Holy Spirit, according to her *Vita*. It was "a place where the river Nahe flows into the Rhine, a hill dedicated in days of old to the name of St. Rupert the confessor."[5] Certainly she also appreciated that her new women's cloister would be located near the large town of Bingen on the Rhine, which placed it at a very exposed position along the main transportation route of the Middle Ages. The monks of Disibodenberg, especially Abbot Kuno, had a very different perspective. The fame of their *magistra* had brought them much income, which their monastery could not and did not want to do without. Fearing not only of the departure of the seer but also the elimination of the dowries of the aristocratic sisters, they opposed this plan. In this tense situation, Hildegard cleverly used her family relations to gain the support of Archbishop Heinrich of Mainz. At the same time, she was afflicted by a debilitating disease, which she attributed to the fact that the fulfillment of the divine will (this was not about her personal will) had been delayed. Her *Vita* reports that Abbot Kuno, who did not believe she was ill,

> *went in to see for himself. He tried with all his strength to raise her head, or to move her with a lever onto her side, but for all his efforts he accomplished nothing. He was so astonished at the strange phenomenon, that he concluded this was no ordinary human illness, but rather a divine chastisement. From then on, he would not offer any more opposition to the divine decree, lest he himself incur something worse.*[6]

After Hildegard obtained the consent of the skeptical Kuno for her plan in this way, she became—as her *Vita* reports— healthy again and was able to get up from her sickbed.

With the help of her sponsors, Archbishop Heinrich and Richardis of Stade (the mother of her fellow sister with the same name), Hildegard eventually acquired the property at the Rupertsberg. The construction of the convent began and in 1150 Hildegard and eighteen of her sisters moved into the new foundation. Like the Disibodenberg, the Rupertsberg too remained a construction site for quite some time.

However, the struggle for legal and financial independence from the Disibodenberg monks continued. By 1155 Hildegard was able to secure exclusive rights to the property at the Rupertsberg. Three years later, Heinrich's successor, Archbishop Arnold of Mainz, again guaranteed protection for the new foundation and regulated the temporal and spiritual relations between the Disibodenberg and the Rupertsberg women's cloister (for this reason, the Disibodenberg monks were obliged to provide the nuns with a chaplain from among their number). During the negotiations about dowries, compensation and the independence of the new cloister, the health of the seer changed again and again according to the level of success or failure of her plans. Finally, Hildegard waived most of the dowry of the former Disibodenberg sisters and received as compensation the protection of the Archbishop of Mainz, as well as an extensive legal independence from the Disibodenberg monks. Despite this deprivation, the Rupertsberg became a fairly wealthy convent.

Guibert of Gembloux described the "miracle" of the Rupertsberg monastery in a letter from 1177:

> Though this monastery was founded but recently—a short space of time ago, that is twenty-seven years—not by any of the emperors or bishops or the powerful or the rich of any region, but by a woman who was poor, a stranger, and sick; yet it has made such progress in its religious character and in its resources that it is skilfully laid out, not with grand but with commodious and dignified buildings most suitable for a religious community, with running water distributed through all the workshops. Furthermore, not counting guests whom we are never without, and the administrators of the house of which they have several, the monastery provides enough for the expenses of food and clothing of fifty sisters without any shortfall.

Guibert admired the "beauty of peace and of all delight and pleasantness" in which the mother embraces her daughters with such love, and the daughters submit to the mother with such awe, "that it is hard to decide whether the mother surpasses the daughters in this eagerness or the daughters their mother." About the *magistra*, he writes:

Hildegard's Monastery on the Marian Wing of the Isenheim Altar
by Matthias Grünewald, 1512/16

*She gives the requested advice to you; she solves difficult questions
that she is asked; she writes books, teaches her sisters, helps sinners
who come to her, and is thus completely and fully preoccupied all
the time.*[7]

According to the convent's annals whereby the successor
of Saint Hildegard is still the "Abbess of Rupertsberg and
Eibingen," in 1165 Hildegard founded a second convent in
Eibingen on the other side of the Rhine; in this convent she
also admitted less well-off and non-aristocratic so-called
"lay-sisters."

STAGE 9

The Bingen Hildegard Way

9

The Bingen Hildegard Way

Length 4.8 – 1.5 hrs. – Ascending 57 m – easy

The ninth stage of the Hildegard Way is a walk through the city of Bingen. One could also say that the Hildegard Way merges here with the Bingen Hildegard Way, which the Cultural Office of the City of Bingen has marked as a tour to the most important Hildegard sites in Bingen and Bingerbrück. We recommend that all Hildegard pilgrims go to all the places where Hildegard tableaux are located: at the Rupertsberg (**Tableau 56** and **57**), the "Museum am Strom" (**Tableau 58**), and the Rochusberg (**Tableau 59**).

The Bingen Hildegard Way begins at the "Museum am Strom" (Museum on the Rhine), with its permanent Hildegard-Exhibition (since 2014) and its Hildegard Garden, now simply

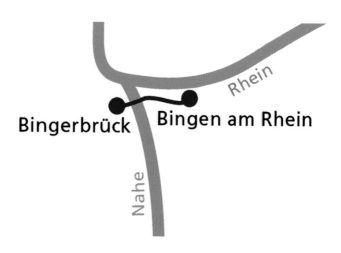

View from the Rupertsberg across the Nahe River to Bingen town with the Basilica St. Martin to the left and Klopp Castle to the right

called "Hildegarden." There is also **Tableau 58** on the Hildegard Way which tells about the Hildegard City of Bingen.

From there, the Bingen Hildegard Way invites us for a tour along the numbered stations 1–16. Besides historical sites, the tour also includes the "Hildegard Information Point," shops and restaurants that identify with Hildegard or that offer Hildegard products—from literature to wine to spices or teas. Moreover, there are history projectors that offer visitors computer-generated images of the lost monastery on the Rupertsberg.

Carved altar with vital image of St. Hildegard in the St. Rochus Chapel from 1895 (right, top); St. Rupert and St. Hildegard Church in Bingen-Bingerbrück (right, bottom)

271

View from Bingen across the Nahe River to the Rupertsberg. Arcades of Hildegard's Cloister Church are underneath the white villa to the left.

In their search for Hildegard's Bingen abbey, many Hildegard friends from all over the world first arrive at the nineteenth-century neo-Romanesque St. Rupert and Saint Hildegard Church. This church contains relics of the saint, namely an elbow in a golden shrine. In addition to its beautiful interior, the church has very recently been equipped with a laser-show and thus turned into a center for Hildegard pilgrims.

In front of the church, there is a Hildegard sculpture by Karl-Heinz Oswald and an information tableau about Hildegard's late visionary work (**Tableau 56**, "*Liber Divinorum Operum*").

The actual site where Hildegard built her monastery is a little below at "Am Rupertsberg 16," a less attractive address with a tanning salon and a computer store. The tableau about "The Ruperts-

Heilige Hildegard. Bronze sculpture by Karl-Heinz Oswald, 2012.

berg Women's Monastery" (**Tableau 57**) is below, with a view to where the Nahe River flows into the Rhine and where one can see the city of Bingen on the other side. Looking down to the railroad tracks then tells us what happened to the ruins after the monastery was burned down in 1632 during the Thirty Years' War: they were deliberately blown up in 1857 in order to build the Naheland railway.

However, one can discover remains of the old monastery. There are remains of arches of the old cloister church in the villa "*Herterhaus*"; they were discovered in 1976 when the villa burned down and had to be renovated. Also, in 1998, the owner of the entire site renovated the vaults at some expense. Since 2009, this Rupertsberg Vault (*Gewölbekeller*) has been leased to the Rupertsberg Hildegard Society; in the spirit of Hildegard, this society organizes events and seeks to keep the vault open for visitors. Nevertheless, on most days, an advance notification is recommended (www.rupertsberger-hildegard-gesellschaft.de).

The way from the Rupertsberg to the Rochusberg is quite long, and some might prefer to drive. In either case, it is worth the visit. What awaits the pilgrim is not only the St. Rochus Chapel, which can be seen from far in the Rhine Valley; but also, what is possibly the most aesthetically, ecologically, and culinarily enjoyable place on the whole Hildegard

Concert by Scivias quartet from Barcelona in St. Hildegard Church in Bingen

Evening meditation in the Rupertsberg vault in Bingen (above); the author in front of tableau 57, The Rupertsberg Women's Monastery (right)

Way, namely, the Hildegard Forum of the Sisters of the Cross (*Kreuzschwestern*). Here is also the last tableau of the Hildegard Way (**Tableau 59**, "After Hildegard's Death").

In the nineteenth century, the St. Rochus Chapel became one of the most important sites for Hildegard veneration in Bingen; this was because in that time of secularization, the Eibingen monastery was dissolved and the Bingen Brothers of St. Rochus acquired for their chapel its interior furnishings as well as the relics of St. Rupert (the relics of St. Hildegard remained in the Eibingen parish church). Unfortunately, in 1889 a fire destroyed a large part of this interior. The late Gothic canopied altar that we see today was not created until 1895 for the Rochus Chapel by the Busch family, who were woodcarvers. The St. Rochus Chapel and the yearly St. Rochus Feast in August are of great importance for the city of Bingen. There are also many worship services in Bingen, and weddings often are celebrated afterwards in the Hildegard Forum. The architecture of this newly constructed ecological forum resembles "Hildegard's cosmic wheel laid down on earth"; and everything is inviting to the inside and outside, with an open design: the herbal garden with a fountain in front of the house and the terrace with an orchard behind the house; a bookstore

274

with Hildegard products and a Hildegard exhibition inside; Hildegard menus and Hildegardian spices such as galangal and thyme in the restaurant area. Almost every Saturday there are conferences, weddings or birthday parties with music. And since 2015, the Hildegard Forum operates its own hotel. With all that, this establishment won a prize in 2005 for its exemplary employment of disabled people. It is simply a pleasure to be here!

The text of the day is about Hildegard's time in Bingen up to her death (1150–1179).

Wall in the Hildegard Forum on the Rochusberg in Bingen

Herbal garden with fountain at the Hildegard Forum

TABLEAU 56

Liber Divinorum Operum

St. Rupert and St. Hildegard Church, Bingerbrück

"The Human Being in the Cosmos," *Liber Divinorum Operum* I.2

Saint Hildegard was in her seventies when she completed her last work, the *Liber Divinorum Operum* (*Book of Divine Works*) in 1173. The first part explores the intricate physical and spiritual relationships between the cosmos and the human person with the famous image of the Universal Man standing astride the cosmic spheres. The second part examines the rewards for virtue and the punishments for vice. At the end of each, Hildegard writes extensive commentaries on the Prologue to John's Gospel and the first chapter of Genesis. She is the only known pre-modern woman to have done so. Finally, the third part tells the history of salvation imagined as the City of God standing next to the mountain of God's foreknowledge with divine love (*caritas*) reigning over all.

For Hildegard, the Incarnation of the Word as Jesus Christ is the key moment of all history. God willed from eternity that his Son would become a human being to complete his work. Humankind shares in God's creative capacity and loving mission. We are, after all, made in his image—for Hildegard, the tunic of the incarnate Christ; and we are made in his likeness—the rationality of the Word that creates and loves. We contain all creation within ourselves and we are divinely called to co-operate in the Creator's work. The scope of Hildegard's visionary theology is both cosmic and close—reflections of God's loving revelation of himself are both grand and utterly intimate as the work of God reaches from the very heart of infinity down into every smallest detail of the created world.

Nathaniel Campbell

TABLEAU 57

The Rupertsberg Women's Monastery

Rupertsberg

**Hildegard's Monastery on the Bingen Rupertsberg.
Mural relief at St. Hildegard's Church.**

Though this monastery was founded but recently—a short space of time ago, that is twenty seven years—not by any of the emperors or bishops or the powerful or the rich of any region, but by a woman who was poor, a stranger, and sick; yet it has made such progress in its religious character and in its resources that it is skilfully laid out, not with grand but with commodious and dignified buildings most suitable for a religious community, with running water distributed through all the workshops.

Guibert of Gembloux, 1177[1]

Hildegard's fame as a seeress had already preceded her when in 1150/1152 she moved with nineteen of her sisters from the Disibodenberg to the Rupertsberg. Even though at the age of fifty-two, she was already considered to be an old woman, the busiest time of her life was only beginning. At first, she was occupied with the new construction of the Rupertsberg monastery. As the Disibodenberg monks did not want to release the urgently-needed dowry of her sisters, she had to search for other sponsors and ultimately was successful.

Under the assistance of the monk Volmar and the nun Richardis of Stade, she finally completed her first work, *Scivias*, in the new Rupertsberg scriptorium. In 1151, she began to work on her medical writing (*Liber Physica* and *Causae et Curae*). Her ethical book (*Liber Vitae Meritorum*) followed in 1158.

The central position of the monastery on the Rhine drew many visitors. Also, Hildegard was occupied with her extensive correspondence from all over the world, and the "trumpet of God" was invited to speak in person in many locations. Thus, she did not merely speak in monasteries but also preached in cathedrals and at public places, such as Mainz, Trier, Cologne, Kirchheimbolanden and Hirsau.

In the time between 1163 und 1173, she was occupied with her latest mystical work (*Liber Divinorum Operum*).

In 1165, according to the convent's history, Hildegard also acquired a second convent in Eibingen and assumed leadership of it.

In 1177, at the end of her life, the Walloon monk Guibert of Gembloux visited the nunnery and admired the peaceful atmosphere and the loving relations between daughters and mother.

On September 17, 1179 Hildegard of Bingen died in her Rupertsberg Monastery.

Rainbow seen at the Rochusberg in Bingen on the Rhine

O Jerusalem—Sequence for Saint Rupert

Jerusalem! Royal city,
walls of gold and purple banners,

building of utmost bounty,
light never darkened,

lovely at dawn,
ablaze at noon.

Blessed be your childhood
that glimmers at dawn,
praised be your vigor
that burns in the sun.

O Rupert! Pearl
of the morning, diamond
at noon, ever sparkling!
Fools cannot hide you,
nor the vale the mountain.

Jerusalem! In the frames
of your windows glisten your
gems,
lapis lazuli and topaz,
Rupert among them,
a light never quenched
. . .
In your soul the Spirit's
symphonies ring, you sing
with angels, join their carols,
Christ your radiance,
pure your song.

Chalice of honor! Child
and youth, you sighed
after God, feared and embraced
him
whose bounty lured yours
like a rare perfume.

O Jerusalem! Founded
on glowing stones, shooting
starts, sheep lost and found:
Christ called and publicans raced,
sinners made haste
to your walls to be laid in their
place.

Like clouds they coursed
through the skies, the living
stones, on wings of goodwill,
to gleam in your walls.

. . .

Hear, o crowned ones,
O radiant-gowned ones,
you who dwell in Jerusalem!
and Rupert, helper and friend,
remember and send
for your servants in exile
when exile has end.

Hildegard of Bingen[2]

TABLEAU 58

Bingen, the Hildegard-Town

"Museum am Strom," Bingen

Bingen on the Rhine

Hildegard's decision in 1150 to leave the Disibodenberg and found her own monastery in Bingen was a decisive moment in her life: It meant that the activities of the prophetess were no longer limited by the cloistered walls, but instead, in the following twenty-five years, Hildegard took on a nearly public role as a much in-demand author and counsellor.

An example of this is the extensive exchange of letters she had with correspondents from all over Europe. The newly-chosen site in Bingen was of great importance in this regard; as an important junction of old Roman roads at the confluence of the Rhine and Nahe Rivers, it enabled the connection to the major communication networks of the era.

Around 1150, when the founding of today's metropolises such as Munich and Berlin was still forthcoming, Bingen was one of the first towns along the Rhine that already had a truly urban character. For centuries, there had been a marketplace, and the merchants of Bingen engaged in long-distance trade with cities such as Koblenz and Trier. The Bingen market was connected to the economic "lifeline" of the Rhine by the *Salzgasse*, which was already documented by then; this is a clear hint to the early importance of the profitable salt-trade.

By having its own court, the town also set itself apart legally from the surrounding villages. The citizens already regulated important aspects of public life on their own: from a 1160 document, we know that the city raised taxes from its inhabitants. With this money, major communal projects were financed, such as the construction and maintenance of the city wall.

From Hildegard's *Vita*, we learn that the citizens of Bingen celebrated the arrival of the prophetess at the Rupertsberg with exuberance: "For ahead of her in the town of Bingen and nearby villages, there were many of distinguished rank as well as no small number of common folk, all of whom went out to welcome her, with much dancing and singing of the divine praises."[3]

Due to the lack of sources, it is barely ascertainable today as to what Hildegard's town looked like. We may assume only a rudimentary ideal image as is depicted here.

Matthias Schmandt

TABLEAU 59

After Hildegard's Death

St. Rochus Chapel on the Rochusberg, Bingen

Vital image of St. Hildegard in the St. Rochus Chapel, 1895

Already during her lifetime, Hildegard of Bingen (1098–1179) had become known as prophetess of the Rhine in the entire empire. After her death, her veneration as a saint began and, in 1233, Pope Gregory IX initiated the process of her canonization. Even though this process was not successful in the following centuries, many people streamed to the monastery and its chapel, in which an image of the Virgin Mary was venerated. In the centuries until the time of the Reformation, Hildegard was mainly known for her apocalyptic preaching.

After the Rupertsberg monastery was destroyed in the Thirty Years' War in 1632 and the Eibingen convent became its legal successor, difficult years began and Hildegard's work was nearly forgotten—except by her sisters. When, in 1803, the Eibingen convent was closed down in the course of secularization, all its possessions were lost and its monastic life ended. During the German cultural struggle (*Kulturkampf*) of the nineteenth century, the Bingen Rochus Chapel became the new site of Catholic Hildegard veneration. Today's St. Hildegard Abbey was built in 1900–1904 in neo-Romanesque style.

The sisters embarked on theological and historical Hildegard studies, and, in 1927–1933, they produced a complete facsimile copy of the illuminated Rupertsberg *Liber Scivias*; this was a fortunate occurrence because the medieval original was lost in World War II. During the Nazi regime, on July 2, 1941, the Gestapo expelled the 115 sisters from their nunnery. Only with their return on July 2, 1945 (!), could they take up their work again; this now included editing and translating all of Hildegard's work.

Due to Hildegard's 800th anniversary of her death in 1979, and also the 900th anniversary of her birth in 1998, more and more was published about the German woman mystic, physician, composer, and prophetess worldwide and many people expected her soon to be canonized. Yet, this occurred only in 2012: German Pope Benedict XVI canonized Hildegard of Bingen on Pentecost Monday, May 10, and on October 7 of the same year, he also declared her as *Doctor Ecclesiae Universalis*; she is only the fourth woman amongst thirty-one male Doctors of the Church.

Sixth Station
in Hildegard's Life:
The Bingen Period

by Annette Esser

In addition to the foundation and concern for her two convents, the *magistra* also continued with her literary activities. With the help of Volmar, Richardis, and other nuns, she was able to complete her first book, *Scivias* (*Know the Ways*), in the Rupertsberg scriptorium; it included the famous illuminations.[4]

Then in 1151 she started to work on a major scientific and medical encyclopedia, the *Liber Subtilitatum Diversarum Naturarum Creaturum Simplicis Medicinae* (*Nine Books on the Subtleties of Different Kinds of Creatures*). This book is known as the *Physica* and includes a comprehensive herbal, a bestiary and a lapidary, but it lacks a foreword. Hildegard supplemented this *Book of Simple Medicine* with her *Book of Compound Medicine*; this handbook is known as *Causae et Curae* and is about diseases and their treatment. Unlike *Physica*, it is not written in the systematic style, but rather in the style of a journal, yet it offers Hildegard's original and rich descriptions of human sexuality.

In 1158, Hildegard began the second volume of her theology, the *Liber Vitae Meritorum* (*Book of Life Merits*), which she finished in 1163. It describes virtues and vices, and contains Hildegard's ethics.

Her third and final visionary work, *Liber Divinorum Operum* or *De Operatione Dei* (*World and Man*), occupied her time from 1163 to 1173.

At the same time, she was busy composing liturgical texts and songs. Her musical drama *Ordo Virtutum* and seventy-five of her songs, the *Symphonia Armoniae Celestium Revelationum*, make her one of the most important composers in all of music history, even though she could not write musical notation (*Neumen*):

> But I have also written songs with melodies in praise of God and the Saints without instruction from any human being, and I have sung them though I have never learned musical notation or any kind of singing.[5]

Hildegard's correspondence extended over three decades from 1147 until her death. She wrote to people of all social classes, to popes, emperors, abbots and abbesses, prelates, priests, monks, nuns and lay people, especially women. It seems that her correspondents strongly desired to receive her letters, because they were convinced that through the mouth of the prophetess God himself spoke directly to them.

One example is her letter to Guibert of Gembloux. This ardent Walloon monk had written to her first in 1175 with a mixture of admiration and curiosity, requesting that she give him some information about her visionary experiences. In a further letter he had attached a catalogue of thirty-nine more or less subtle questions that he had devised with his monks. Yet when he finally received a response from the famous seer, he did not dare to open it immediately, but he first went

> ". . . into the nearest church, put Hildegard's letter on the altar and prayed fervently to the Holy Spirit for a worthy condition of his heart. Then he took the letter, read it twice, three times in silence and admiration, and almost fell into ecstasy." On the following day "he read the letter aloud at an assembly of clergy and laity. The former Abbot Rupert of Königstal, a Premonstratensian Abbey in

the diocese of Toul, sat there during the entire reading, cradled his head thoughtfully and then exclaimed enthusiastically that these words could come from no one other than the Holy Spirit. The most astute masters from France could not have produced done such a work. . . . With their dry hearts and puffed-up cheeks they make a big noise, yet lose themselves in investigations and disputes. . . . But this godly woman . . . only emphasizes the one thing that is necessary, namely, the glory of the threefold God. She draws on an inner fullness and pours it out to quench the thirst of the thirsty."[6]

In political affairs as well, Hildegard was a much sought-after correspondent. She knew how to take advantage of her aristocratic position for herself and her monastic foundations, and she also did not shy away from harsh criticism. The most outstanding example is her ambivalent relation to Frederick Barbarossa, which Barbara Newman calls "a double-edged relationship." After the emperor was elected on March 4, 1152, he invited the famous seer from nearby Rupertsberg to his palace in Ingelheim in the early summer of 1154, that is, shortly before his coronation in Rome. We are not informed about the content of their conversation, but in 1163 he granted Rupertsberg an edict of imperial protection in perpetuity. However, when the emperor installed a new anti-pope three times in succession, and in so doing, created a schism in the church, on account of which many of Hildegard's episcopal friends suffered, she did not behave like a protégée but instead opposed him. During the first schism, in 1159, when he installed Victor IV against Pope Alexander III, she did not take a stand. Yet when the emperor installed a second anti-pope, Paschal III, in 1164, Hildegard sent him a sharp rebuke by comparing him to a "child and a madman." After the death of that pope in 1164, when Barbarossa stubbornly dared to support a third anti-pope (Callistus III), Hildegard hurled the wrath of God against him:

> *He Who Is says: I destroy contumacy, and by myself I crush the*
> *resistance of those who despise me. Woe, woe to the malice of wicked*
> *men who defy me! Hear this, king, if you wish to live; otherwise*
> *my sword shall smite you.*[7]

Still the king remained obdurate and the schism dragged on until 1179.[8] Nevertheless, despite Hildegard's harsh criticism in the name of God, his letter of protection continued to preserve her cloister at the Rupertsberg from all harm during later factional warfare.

Judging from her correspondence, we assume that the prophetess spoke in many monasteries, cathedrals and public places. She went on extended preaching journeys on boats along the Rhine, Main, Neckar and Mosel. Already an old woman over sixty, she did not undertake this simply on her own initiative, but as she herself admits, she was urged to do this by, for example, the dean and the clergy of Cologne Cathedral:

> *Poor little timorous figure of a woman that I am. I have worn*
> *myself out for two whole years so that I might bring this message*
> *on person to the magistrates, teachers, and other wise men who*
> *hold the higher positions in the Church.*[9]

In the nineteenth century, four preaching tours were reconstructed. Even though this compilation is debated today, it still gives an impression of her journeys along the major rivers and of the places where she probably spoke. Accordingly, in 1158 her first journey brought her by boat along the Main River. She preached in monastic communities in Mainz, Wertheim, Würzburg, Kitzingen, Ebrach and Bamberg. In 1160 she embarked on a second journey. This time going south towards Lorraine, she stopped in Metz and Kraufthal; on Pentecost, she preached publicly in the cathedral city of Trier. Her third journey, from 1161 to 1163, led down the Rhine to Boppard, Andernach, Siegburg, Cologne and Werden. The letter that she wrote at the urging of Dean Philip after her visit reflected the tenor of her sermon, in which she literally seemed to read the riot act to her listeners. However, she did not write these things "to the shepherds of the Church" in her own name but in the name of the one "Who was, and is, and is about to come (Rev. 1:4)":

> I set you like the sun and the other luminaries so that you might bring light to people through the fire of doctrine, shining in good reputation and setting hearts ablaze with zeal.

But what do these shepherds do instead, or rather, what do they *not* do? Obstinate and self-willed, they do not proclaim justly the righteousness of God.

> You are the night exhaling darkness, and you are like people who do not work, not even walk in the light because of your indolence. . . . You do not have eyes, since your works do not shine before men with the fire of the Holy Spirit, and you do not meditate on good examples for them. . . . But you are laid low and do not hold up the Church, retreating instead to the cave of your own desire. And because of the tedium brought on by your riches, avarice, and other vain pursuits, you do not properly teach your subordinates, nor indeed do you even allow them to seek instruction from you. . . . You are not presenting a wholesome and stable example of morality before the people. . . . You ought to be the day, but you are the night. . . . You are not the sun and moon and stars in the firmament of God's law and justice. Rather, you are the darkness, in which you lie as if already dead.[10]

After another serious illness lasting from 1167 until 1170, the seeress, now in her seventies, undertook a fourth and final preaching tour in Swabia, visiting Rodenkirchen, Maulbronn, Hirsau, Kirchheim and Zwiefalten.[11]

The last years of her life brought perhaps the most painful test for Hildegard. In 1178, an interdict was imposed on the women's community of the eighty-year-old abbess by the Bishop of Mainz and by his canons. That meant that the nuns were not only forbidden to receive communion, but also to sing in the convent church. The alleged reason for this ban was the burial of an excommunicated nobleman in the Rupertsberg churchyard. The canons of Mainz Cathedral demanded that his bones be exhumed. Hildegard rejected this and instead solemnly blessed the grave with her abbatial staff. One can speculate today about the real religious or political reasons. However, the conflict went on for a year and was not resolved until shortly before Hildegard's death. Only with vehement and continued writings of protest and with the support of Archbishop Phillip of Cologne, did the abbess finally succeed in having the ban repealed in March 1179.

Two points are illustrated in this conflict: first, Hildegard's determination not to give up or give in is impressive, just in order to keep peace in her old age.[12] Second, we owe to this circumstance a unique reference in the history of music. Only because of the interdict did the seer and composer write a long epistle to the prelates of Mainz in which she passionately defends the importance of the liturgical music that is forbidden to her and her nuns under the interdict. Hildegard's wonderful melodic compositions for high female voices already show that tones and sounds do not merely have an earthly dimension for her. Instead, music stands in harmonic relation with the entire cosmos, and by their singing, humans add their voices to the heavenly singing of the choirs of angels.

Consider too that just as the body of Jesus Christ was born of the purity of the Virgin Mary through the operation of the Holy Spirit so too the canticle of praise, reflecting celestial harmony, is rooted in the Church through the Holy Spirit. The body is the vestment of the spirit, which was a living voice, and so it is proper for the body, in harmony with the soul, to use its voice to sing praises to God. Whence, in metaphor, the prophetic spirit commands us to praise God with clashing cymbals and cymbals of jubilation (cf.

Ps 150:5), as well as other musical instruments which men of wisdom and zeal invented, because all arts pertaining to things useful and necessary for mankind have been created by the breath that God sent into man's body. For this reason it is good that God be praised in all things.[13]

Only half a year after the happy end of this conflict, Hildegard died. This is described in her *Vita*:

When the blessed mother had devotedly waged battle for the Lord with many difficult struggles, she felt the weariness of this present life and daily yearned to be dissolved and to be with Christ (Phil 1:23). God graciously heeded her longing, and as it had been her wish, by the spirit of prophecy revealed to her end, which she foretold to her sisters. She had laboured in illness for some time, when in the eighty-second year of her life, on the fifteenth day before the Kalends of October [17 September], she departed with a happy passage to her heavenly spouse. Her daughters, to whom she had been all joy and solace, wept bitterly as they took part in the funeral rites of their beloved mother.[14]

The veneration of Hildegard as a saint began immediately after her death, and Pope Gregory IX initiated the canonization process in 1233. The judgment of William of Auxerre of the Theological Faculty of Paris was sought, and he declared that "Hildegard's writings do not contain human but divine words." Possibly for technical reasons, this process was not completed.

The inquisitors did their work shoddily and failed to record names, dates and places in their account of Hildegard's miracles. . . . Legend has it that the saint's miracles had ceased, because a steady stream of pilgrims had been disturbing the nuns, who asked the bishop if he might order their deceased founder, under obedience, to work no more wonders.[15]

Although Hildegard had been venerated as a saint in the Rhineland for centuries, and, although she is also listed in the *Acta Sanctorum*, the official calendar of saints in the Catholic Church, more than eight hundred years passed after her death before Pope Benedict XVI officially canonized her for the whole Catholic Church on Pentecost Monday, May 10, 2012. On October 7 of the same year, also by the personal intervention of the German pope, Hildegard—the fourth woman after Teresa of Avila, Catherine of Siena and Therese of Lisieux— was declared a Doctor of the Church.

STAGE 10

The Rüdesheim
Hildegard Way

10

The Rüdesheim Hildegard Way

Length 6.8 km – ca. 2 hrs. – Ascent 165 m – Descent 165 m – medium

The tenth stage of the pilgrimage path leads to us to Rüdesheim and Eibingen. After crossing the Rhine with the passenger or car ferry, the so-called Rüdesheim Hildegard Way leads uphill from the popular wine town of Rüdesheim on the Rhine to the parish and pilgrimage church at Eibingen and finally to St. Hildegard's Abbey.

For Hildegard friends from all over the world, the Benedictine Abbey of St. Hildegard is the most important center of attraction.

Yet this magnificent neo-Romanesque building was constructed only in 1904. The monastery that Hildegard had established in Eibingen as a daughter convent—lies a little bit below in the old parish church on Marienthaler Straße. Spiritually,

Benedictine sisters of St. Hildegard's Abbey

this is the real destination of the pilgrimage way. Here, in front of a wonderful wall mosaic that shows Hildegard's vision of the Trinity (*Scivias* II.2), we find Hildegard's shrine with her relics (at least the main part of them). The shrine was crafted in 1929 in the Benedictine Maria Laach Abbey and in Cologne.

A fire that occurred in 1932 spared the shrine, yet it destroyed the remaining church furnishings; this is why the interior of the church looks rather modern today.

Since 2017, the Diocese of Limburg has supported the establishment of a pilgrimage

St. Hildegard's shrine and mosaic of her vision of Trinity in the Pilgrimage Church of Eibingen (right, top); Tableau of the Rüdesheim Hildegard Way (right, bottom)

center. This is for pilgrims on the Hildegard Way as well as from the Rheingau Monastery Way. Over a length of thirty kilometers, this *Klostersteig Rheingau* leads from Eberbach Monastery to the monasteries Johannisberg (today a castle), Marienthal, Nothgottes and St. Hildegard in Eibingen up to St. Mary's Church (*Marienkirche*) in Rüdesheim-Aulhausen.

Those who can or want to spend only a day for a pilgrimage are encouraged to do this on a Saturday in the pilgrimage season from May 10 through October 7. After having visited the pilgrimage church (perhaps for a worship service), they can walk through the vineyard mountains uphill to St. Hildegard's Abbey. There, a store (*Klosterladen*) and a café (*Klostercafé*) invite the pilgrim. A good way to complete the day is to attend vespers at half past five in the afternoon. All other prayer and worship times are to be found on the abbey's website.

Pilgrims who walked the whole Hildegard Way can get their final stamp here and complete their pilgrimage.

In the text of the day, Sr. Philippa Rath, OSB reports on the history of St. Hildegard's Abbey, whose abbess today is the fortieth successor of Saint Hildegard. As there are no meditation or information tableaux on this stage, we finish this chapter with a meditation by Sr. Caecilia Bonn, OSB (1925–2012) and with a song by Hildegard of Bingen about *caritas*, the divine love which fills the cosmos.

Sculpture by Sr. Christophora Janssen, OSB, at St. Hildegard's Abbey

POEM

St. Hildegard of Bingen's Theology

Elected *magistra*

By her fellow sisters

In 1136

Canonized as Saint

By Pope Benedict XVI

On Pentecost Monday, 2012

Promoted On October 7, 2012

As the old and the new

Doctor of the Church

Doctor Ecclesiae

She teaches us

Cosmic

Holistic

Visionary and

Her theology of the feminine

Scivias

A holistic presentation of reality

A clear structure of Christian doctrine

We see the historic significance

In the art of healing

That she practiced

That is generating renewed interest

In today's world

In her version of trying to understand
The synergy
Of God and humans
Working together
In the salvation history
Of humanity
To achieve the realization
Of salvation
To build the City of God
For all humanity.

Karen S. E. Stock

Saint Hildegard's Abbey in Changing Times

by Sr. Philippa Rath, OSB

St. Hildegard's Abbey, situated above Rüdesheim on the Rhine and considered by many to be a Romanesque building, was only built at the beginning of the twentieth century; yet it regards itself as a foundation of Saint Hildegard, which goes back to her old Eibingen convent.

In 1150, Hildegard of Bingen built her first monastery on the Rupertsberg, at the mouth of the Nahe River. As the number of callings steadily increased and more and more young women gathered around her, Hildegard acquired the former Augustinian double convent of Eibingen in 1165 and also undertook the direction of the new Eibingen foundation. After the death of Saint Hildegard, the two convents, Rupertsberg and Eibingen, developed in accordance with the changing course of history: times of prosperity alternated with times of decline.

In the turmoil of the Thirty Years' War, the Rupertsberg monastery was destroyed in 1632 by Swedish troops. The nuns had to escape but returned to the Rupertsberg in 1636. Yet the convent buildings were in such bad condition that a reconstruction seemed impossible. Therefore, the Rupertsberg nuns felt impelled to take refuge in the Eibingen convent. In 1642 the last Rupertsberg abbess, Anna Lerch of Dürmstein, left her office. The following 150 years were marked by many hardships. Famine, plague, wars and devastations affected the Eibingen convent. Then, in the course of secularization in 1803, the convent was suspended and all possessions were lost. Therewith monastic life in Eibingen ceased. The monastic church was taken over by the parish. This is why, to this day, the relics of Saint Hildegard still are venerated in the parish and pilgrimage church of Eibingen. Since 2002, a sister of Saint Hildegard's Abbey has been in charge of the pastoral care of pilgrims there. In this way, the old and the new Eibingen monastery are interrelated again very concretely.

Plan for a New Foundation

The plan for the foundation of a new monastery, which at once was supposed to revitalize the old Eibingen convent and also hearken back to the old Rupertsberg convent that had been destroyed by the Swedish, is due to the efforts of Bishop Peter Josef Blum of Limburg (1842–1883). He and Ludwig Schneider, who was the priest of Eibingen from 1840 to 1864, greatly encouraged the veneration of Saint Hildegard in the nineteenth century. Bishop Blum, who had lost his bishop's seat in the German cultural conflict (*Kulturkampf*) during the years 1876–1883, was granted asylum by Prince Karl of Löwenstein-Wertheim-Rosenberg at Haid Castle in Bohemia. Blum's successor, Bishop Dr. Karl Klein, was also closely connected to the princely family and from the very beginning inspired them with his plans to revitalize the old Eibingen monastery. The prince took up the idea enthusiastically, because in this way he wished to restore the secularized church's possessions that had come to his family as a result of the 1802 political decision (*Reichsdeputationshauptschluss*). As a consequence, his oldest daughter, Benedicta, nun of St. Cecilia's Abbey in Solesmes, France, was to become the first abbess of the new foundation. When she died unexpectedly at the age of only thirty-six on July 2, 1896, he still stuck with his plan and did not shy away from financial and personal sacrifice for the re-establishment of the monastery.

St. Hildegard's Abbey was built on the hill above the village of Eibingen. The building material—sandstone interfused by quartzite—came from rock above the construction site. The

Sisters at St. Hildegard's Abbey in 1904

planning and realization of the new building was under the direction of P. Ludger Rincklake, a monk from the Maria Laach Abbey who had formerly been an architect.

On July 2, 1900, the foundation stone of the new monastery was laid by Archabbot Placidus Wolter of Beuron, who had come to the Rhine representing Bishop Dominikus Willi, who was ill.

The Beginning of Monastic Life

After four years, the monumental building was mostly completed. On September 17, 1904, fourteen Benedictine nuns from St. Gabriel in Prague, the first women's convent of the Beuron congregation, moved into the new foundation. By two

The abbey's library painted in the Beuron art style

decrees of Pope Leo XIII in 1908, the monastery was elevated to an Abbey and endowed with all privileges of the former convent of Saint Hildegard. As an "exempt" abbey, it is not subordinate to the local bishop but rather directly immediately to the Holy See. On September 7, 1908, the painting of the church by P. Paulus Krebs, Beuron, and his students had progressed so far that the church could be consecrated by Bishop Dominikus Willi.

On the day after the consecration, the prioress, Regintrudis Sauter, was ordained as the first abbess of the monastic community. Thus, she was the thirty-sixth successor of St. Hildegard, under whose special protection the abbey and the minster were given.

In the following years the number of sisters increased steadily. With God's help and thanks to a wise leadership by the house, the community survived World War I (1914–1918) and the time after the war relatively well. In the postwar period (1918–1939), the eastern wing of the abbey, hitherto merely a shell, was finally completed. The novices' wing and the chapter house moved into this space.

St. Hildegard's Abbey during World War II

The Nazi era and World War II brought severe trials to the monastic community of St. Hildegard's Abbey. Already in May 1941, Abbess Regintrudis Sauter made available part of the abbey as a military hospital with twenty sisters for nursing the wounded and also for army administration, hoping with these actions to save the abbey from closure. This hope was not fulfilled. On July 2, 1941, on the forty-first anniversary of the laying of the abbey's foundation stone, the expulsion of the 115 nuns by the Secret State Police (*Gestapo*) took place. The sisters had to leave their convent, and the monastic possessions were expropriated.

The largest part of the community was taken in by institutions of the order, such as in the congregations of Waldbreibach and Dernbsch and amongst the sisters of Borromeo in Bingen. The Eibingen sisters worked in the hospitals of these communities and did other work there in the remaining years of the war. A small part of the convent remained in St. Hildegard Abbey in order to nurse the wounded as Red Cross Sisters or in order to do the domestic work of the military hospital with its 100 to 130 wounded. In November 1944, Rüdesheim was mostly destroyed by a bombing, yet the monastery remained intact. Since the main military hospital and the operation room in Eibingen had been bombed, the number of beds in the hospital part of Eibingen was increased to 325. A few weeks before the end of the war, on March 19, 1945, the hospital in Eibingen monastery was dissolved. A few days later American troops marched into Rüdesheim. Soon after that, the restitution of the property to its owners was carried out. In part of the building, older citizens of Rüdesheim who had become homeless because of the bombardment of Rüdesheim, found asylum for ten years, as did refugees from the eastern territories of Germany.

The Development of the Abbey after 1945

Up until July 2, 1945—again the anniversary of the foundation—the buildings had been restored sufficiently by some sisters who had already returned, and by many voluntary workers, so that the last expelled sisters could return home. On July 2, monastic life resumed under the guidance of Abbess Regintrudis Sauter—who was by then eighty years old, but still active. Many young women now asked for admission into the abbey; with the resulting steady increase, the inner building of the community could also be restarted. In place of the bells that had been confiscated during the war, on July 1, 1952, four new bells were blessed by Abbot Basileus Ebel from Maria Laach.

On August 4, 1955, ninety-year-old Abbess Regintrudis Sauter resigned after forty-seven years in the position. On August 8, Fortuna Fischer was elected as her successor. On

The abbey church at the event of the inauguration of the new abbess on August 2, 2016

September 17, 1955, she received the ordination for her office from the suffragan bishop Walther Kampe from Limburg. Abbess Fortuna Fischer's tenure was shaped by some essential innovations. In 1967, the formerly separate convents of canonesses and lay sisters were united into one community. According to Vatican II reforms, the altar space and the nuns' choir of the church were redesigned. Both were finalized in the consecration of the altar on September 7, 1967. In the following years the new organ was installed. The high wrought-iron fences that so far had marked the border of the cloister between the choir and the church as well as in the consultation rooms were taken away.

On August 8, 1978, Abbess Fortuna Fischer resigned from office. On August 17, Sr. Edeltraud Forster assumed the position by election of the community and thus became the thirty-eighth successor of St. Hildegard. She was ordained as abbess on September 15, 1978, by Bishop Dr. Wilhelm Kempf from Limburg. One of the most important events of her time in office was May 5, 1988. On this day ten sisters of the Eibingen convent settled in the former Cistercian Marienrode Abbey and revived a long monastic tradition in Lower Saxony after a 180-year interruption. And so, eighty-four years after the re-establishment of St. Hildegard's Abbey, Benedictine life and the spiritual and intellectual world of Saint Hildegard have born fruits again. Ten years later, on May 5, 1998, the daughter convent Marienrode was given its independence. In the same year, on September 21, 1998, after the end of the jubilee year of Saint Hildegard's 900th birthday, Abbess Edeltraud Förster resigned from office for reasons of age. Sr. Gisela Happ was then elected as prioress-administrator on October 1.

Fresco of St. Hildegard in St. Hildegard's Abbey Church, which was also shown at the event of her declaration as Doctor of the Church at St. Peter's Place in Rome

On October 23, 2000, Sr. Clementia Killewald was elected as abbess and thus as the thirty-ninth follower of Saint Hildegard. She received her ordination from bishop Dr. Franz Kamphaus from Limburg. Her motto was: *Dominus ipse faciet* ("The Lord will provide it").

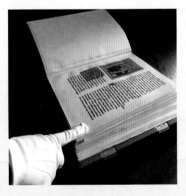

Beginning of the *Liber Scivias*. "Substitute Original" in St. Hildegard's Abbey, 1927–33.

Abbess Clementia's tenure was marked by important and externally visible events. These included the construction of a new guesthouse, art studios, a new shop, an information room, an art cellar and a café, all part of a ten-year project, as well as the establishment of a society of friends in 2001 and a foundation (*Klosterstiftung Sankt Hildegard*) in 2009.

The summit of her time in office was the long-desired official canonization of Hildegard of Bingen on May 10, 2012, and the declaration of Hildegard as a Doctor of the Church on October 7, 2012. This process had gone on for centuries. Abbess Clementia and several sisters of the abbey were significantly involved in its successful completion.

Much too early, the thirty-ninth successor of Saint Hildegard died on July 2, 2016. On August 2, 2016, the convent elected Dorothea Flandera as the new, fortieth abbess of Rupertsberg and Eibingen. The ordination of the abbess was conducted by Bishop Dr. Georg Bätzing on October 3, 2016. Abbess Dorothea offered her service under the motto: *Dominus ipse est* ("It is the Lord").

"As during Hildegard's death a sign appeared in heaven."
Fresco in St. Hildegard's Abbey.

SONG

Talking with Hildegard

One should have wings
all around full of eyes
in which the tear of desire still stands
like a hidden gate
in the circling wheel of eternity.

One should be able to tremble like a harp
touched tenderly by the wind passing by
blow someone else's sound—like a trumpet in the streets of
the town
just so that the guards rub their eyes
facing the splendid light
that begins to sound.

I want to crackle like wood
in the growing fire
whose flame is not silent
because the glow is at work.

You kneel in the fresh wounds of mass
in front of which the angel sinks to silence—
sparkling like a gemstone
in the sun
not knowing
that you to the mouth of the earth
you are giving the kiss of her Creator.

You will blossom
like a rose
that does not know the shadow of falling leaves
because it lives from being embraced.

A reflective surface
in which my beloved one
finds his face
like aroma from the finest spices.

I want to drink from the well
that springs from the Father's heart
and bedews the open earth
with the abundance of fruits . . .
"I am the flower of the field"
the living light speaks—
"the work is mine."

"Caritas – Love," *Liber Divinorum Operum* III.5

We dive into the foaming sea
of heaven's powers
that build the walls
with streets of fire and glass.

As children in innocence
look through windows of faith
with their noses firmly pressed to the glass
uttering an amazed O.
"How good—O how good is God."

We—clumps of earth—
wake up in the heart of the father
as beneath the warm wings of the hen
it is enough to love
to look
and to embrace.

Like a little downy feather
not to be defeated by the sword—
I want to dance in the wind
shedding one's own gravity
held only by God's hands.

Sr. Caecilia Bonn, OSB[1]

Notes

Foreword

1. *Scivias* is an abbreviation for *scito vias Domini* or *scito vias lucis* and means "know the ways of the Lord" or "know the ways of the Living light."

Stage 1

1. Latin text and notes in *Lieder*, 32–34; English translation in *Symphonia*, 115.

2. Petra Urban, *Das Leben ist ein Abenteuer oder gar nichts. Spirituelle Frauengeschichten* (Münsterschwarzach: Vier Türme, 2011) 31–33 (own translation from the German).

3. Hildegard was born in 1098 sometime before September 17. On the day she died, Hildegard was already in her eighty-second year.

4. The exact birthplace of Hildegard is not known for certain. The oldest record by Abbot Trithemius of Sponheim (1462–1516) mentions the castle of Böckelheim. Sr. Marianna Schrader, OSB, concluded that the mention of a Hildebert von Bermersheim hints at the village of Bermersheim in Rheinhessen (1940). In contrast, historian Josef Heinzelmann put forward the theory that Niederhosenbach, a village between Kirn and Idar-Oberstein, could be Hildegard's birthplace (1997). Recently Prof. Dr. Rainer Berndt, SJ, named Bermersheim again in the official booklet on Hildegard's canonization and declaration as Doctor of the Church (*Arbeitshilfe* 2013).

5. Cf. *Beuys*, 36–37; Hildegard's letter to Tengswich of Andernach, in *Correspondence*, 26–28.

6. *Beuys*, 39.

7. *Biographical Sources*, 158–59.

8. *Newman*, 6–7.

Stage 2

1. Latin text and notes in *Lieder*, 180–81; English translation in *Symphonia*, 101.

2. Latin text and notes in *Lieder*, 179–180; English translation in *Newman*, 64.

3. Emerson/Moore and Stefan Morent, according to own notes during a lecture at the International Hildegard Conference in Mainz, March 28, 2013.

4. Marianna Schrader and Adelgundis Führkötter, *Die Echtheit des Schrifttums der heiligen Hildegard von Bingen: Quellenkritische Untersuchungen*, Beihefte zum Archiv für Kulturgeschichte 6 (Köln, Graz: Böhlau, 1956).

5. Quoted according to own notes during a lecture by Sr. Maura Zátonyi on September 29, 2013.

6. Liselotte E. Sauma-Jeitsch, "Die Rupertsberger 'Scivias'-Handschrift: Überlegungen zu ihrer Entstehung," in *Miniaturen*, 12.

7. Quoted according to own record of the lecture of Sr. Maura Zátonyi, OSB, on September 29, 2013.

Stage 3

1. Latin text and notes in *Lieder*, 131–132; English translation by Annette Esser.

2. *Correspondence*, 24.

Stage 4

1. Latin text and notes in *Lieder*, 76–79; English translation in *Symphonia*, 157.

2. *Biographical Sources*, 67.

3. In most literature, Hildegard's kinship to Jutta is assumed, yet it is not proved.

4. *Biographical Sources*, 68.

5. *Biographical Sources*, 70.

6. *Biographical Sources*, 53.

7. *Beuys*, 79.

8. *Biographical Sources*, 77.

Stage 5

1. Latin text and notes in *Lieder*, 61; English translation in *Symphonia*, 143.

2. Latin text and notes in *Lieder*, 194; English translation in *Symphonia*, 253.

3. Latin text and notes in *Lieder*, 69–72; English translation in *Symphonia*, 151.

4. Latin text and notes in *Lieder*, 173; English translation in *Symphonia*, 251.

5. *Biographical Sources*, 81.

6. *Biographical Sources*, 139.

7. "O Ecclesia," in *Symphonia*, 240–241.

8. *Biographical Sources*, 170.

9. Pastor *Johannes Schmelzeis* from Eibingen formulated this in 1879 at the time when there was no convent.

10. *Biographical Sources*, 70.

11. *Biographical Sources*, 80.

Stage 6

1. Latin text and notes in *Lieder*, 22–23; English translation in *Symphonia*, 105.

2. *Biographical Sources*, 141.

3. *Biographical Sources*, 159–60.

4. *Biographical Sources*, 141.

5. *Correspondence*, 27.

6. *Correspondence*, 31.

7. *Biographical Sources*, 142–43.

8. *Biographical Sources*, 144.

9. *Scivias*, 59.

Stage 7

1. Latin text and notes in *Lieder*, 187–188; English translation in *Symphonia*, 135.

2. *Biographical Sources*, 68–69.

3. Interpretation by *Barbara Newman* in *Symphonia*, 127.

4. *Evangelisches Kirchengesangbuch* No. 262; English translation by Annette Esser.

Stage 8

1. Latin text and notes in *Lieder*, 73–76; English translation in *Symphonia*, 155.

2. English translation in Hildegard von Bingen, "*Ordo Virtutum* (The Play of the Virtues)," in *Nine Medieval Latin Plays*, trans. and ed. Peter Dronke, Cambridge Medieval Classics, vol. 1 (Cambridge and New York: Cambridge University Press, 1994).

3. In 1139, the Second Lateran Council decided—amongst other issues—that monks and nuns should no longer be allowed to pray and to sing together in high mass, which de facto meant the end of most double monasteries in the Holy Roman Empire.

4. *Biographical Sources*, 167.

5. *Biographical Sources*, 144.

6. *Biographical Sources*, 145–46.

7. *Biographical Sources* 102.

Stage 9

1. *Biographical Sources*, 101.

2. *Symphonia*, 193.

3. *Biographical Sources*, 147.

4. The question of when the illuminations were completed and who the artist was is discussed in the text of the day of chapter 2. There is a strong argument that Hildegard supervised the making of the illuminations; there is also an argument to name her as the "artist," in the same way as the composer, and not merely the interpreter, is named as the creator of music.

5. *Beuys*, 278.

6. *Briefwechsel*, 225.

7. *Newman*, 13.

8. In order to end the schism, the Third Lateran Council in 1179 decided that a two-thirds majority vote was necessary to elect a Pope in conclave. This is still the practice today.

9. *Correspondence*, 116.

10. *Correspondence*, 109–113.

11. *Newman*, 12.

12. *Beuys*, 346

13. *Correspondence*, 160–61.

14. *Biographical Sources*, 209.

15. *Newman*, 31.

Stage 10

1. Abtei St. Hildegard, ed., *Hildegard von Bingen. Pilgerbuch*, 1998, 57–59. English translation by Annette Esser.

Bibliography

Primary Sources

The Book of the Divine Works. Translated by Nathaniel M. Campbell. Washington, DC: Catholic University of America Press, 2018.

Geschaut im lebendigen Licht: Die Miniaturen des Liber Scivias. Erklärt und gedeutet von Sr. Hiltrud Gutjahr, OSB, und Sr. Maura Zátonyi, OSB. Benediktinerinnen St. Hildegard, Eibingen. Beuron: Beuroner Kunstverlag, 2011 (quoted as *Miniaturen*).

Hildegard of Bingen: Homilies on the Gospel. Translated with Introduction and Notes by Beverly M. Kienzle. Collegeville, MN: Liturgical Press, 2011.

Hildegard of Bingen: Scivias. Translated by Mother Columba Hart and Jane Bishop. Introduction by Barbara J. Newman. Preface by Caroline Walker Bynum. New York: Paulist Press, 1990 (quoted as *Scivias*).

Hildegard von Bingen. "*Ordo Virtutum* (The Play of the Virtues)." In *Nine Medieval Latin Plays*. Translated and edited by Peter Dronke. Cambridge Medieval Classics, vol. 1. Cambridge and New York: Cambridge University Press, 1994.

Hildegard von Bingen Briefwechsel: Nach den ältesten Handschriften übersetzt und nach den Quellen erläutert. Translated by Adelgundis Führkötter. Salzburg: Otto Müller Verlag, 1965 (quoted as *Briefwechsel*).

Hildegard von Bingen's Physica: The Complete English Translation of Her Classic Work on Health and Healing. Translated from the Latin by Priscilla Throop. Rochester, VT: Healing Arts Press, 1998 (quoted as *Physica*).

Jutta and Hildegard: The Biographical Sources. Translated and edited by Anna Silvas. University Park, PA: Pennsylvania State University Press, 1999 (quoted as *Biographical Sources*).

Lieder. Symphoniae. Hildegard von Bingen Werke, vol. 1. Abtei St. Hildegard, Eibingen, ed. Beuron: Beuroner Kunstverlag 2012 (quoted as *Lieder*).

The Personal Correspondence of Hildegard of Bingen: Selected Letters with an Introduction and Commentary by Joseph L. Baird. Oxford and New York: Oxford University Press, 2006 (quoted as *Correspondence*).

Secrets of God. Writings of Hildegard of Bingen. Selected and translated from the Latin by Sabina Flanagan. Boston and London: Shambhala, 1996.

Symphonia: A Critical Edition of the "Symphonia armonie celestium revelationum" [Symphony of the Harmony of Celestial Revelations]. Introduction, translations and commentary by Barbara Newman. Ithaca, NY: Cornell University Press, 1988 (quoted as *Symphonia*).

Secondary Literature

Beuys, Barbara. *Denn ich bin krank vor Liebe. Das Leben der Hildegard von Bingen*. Munich and Vienna: C. Hanser, 2001 (translated from German by Annette Esser; quoted as *Beuys*).

Boyce-Tillman, June. *The Creative Spirit. Harmonious Living with Hildegard of Bingen*. Harrisburg, PA: Morehouse Publishing, 2001 (quoted as *Newman*)

Esser, Annette, ed. *Die Kirchenlehrerin Hildegard von Bingen*. Publikationen des Scivias-Instituts, vol. 1. Berlin: Berlin epubli GmbH, 2015.

Esser, Annette. *Pilgerbuch. Hildegard von Bingen Pilgerwanderweg*. Bad Kreuznach: Matthias Ess, 2017.

Forster, Edeltraud, and Konvent der Benedikterinnenabtei St. Hildegard, eds. *Hildegard von Bingen: Prophetin durch die Zeiten: Zum 900. Geburtstag*, Freiburg: Herder, 1998.

Fox, Matthew. *Hildegard of Bingen: A Saint for Our Times: Unleashing Her Power in the 21st Century*. Vancouver: Namaste Publishing, 2012.

Keating, Colleen. *Hildegard of Bingen: A Poetic Journey*. Port Adelaide, South Australia: Ginninderra Press, 2019.

Newman, Barbara. *Sister of Wisdom. St. Hildegard's Theology of the Feminine*. Berkeley, CA: University of California Press, 1987 (*Hil-*

degard von Bingen. Schwester der Weisheit. Aus dem Englischen von Annette Esser und Mónica Priester. Frauen—Kultur—Geschichte, vol. 2. Freiburg: Herder, 1995).

Ray, Joyce. *Feathers & Trumpets. A Story of Hildegard of Bingen*. Illustrated by Lisa Greenleaf. Amherst, NH: Apprentice Shop Books, 2014.

Sharratt, Mary. *Illuminations. A Novel of Hildegard of Bingen*. Boston and New York: Houghton Mifflin Harcourt, 2012.

Sterringer, Shanon. *30-Day Journey with St. Hildegard of Bingen*. Minneapolis: Augsburg Fortress, 2019.

Storch, Walburga, ed. *The Windows of Faith: Prayers of Holy Hildegard*. Introduction by Caecilia Bonn, OSB. Translated by Sharon Therese Nemeth. Collegeville, MN: Liturgical Press, 1997.

Waterboer, Eveline. *Als das Wort Gottes erklang: Die theologische Bedeutung des Klangs bei Hildegard von Bingen*. Saarbrücken: Fromm Verlag, 2020.

Zátonyi, Maura. *Hildegard von Bingen*. Zugänge zum Denken des Mittelalters, vol. 8. Münster: Aschendorff Verlag, 2017.

Photo Credits

This special Hildegard pilgrimage book owes so much to the images, especially the visionary images of Hildegard herself. Therefore:

First of all we thank **St. Hildegard Abbey** for the permission to show the 27 visionary images of the *Liber Scivias* (the substitute-original is a calligraphic copy from 1927–1933; the medieval original was lost in World War II): pages 18, 24, 40, 50, 72, 80, 97, 99, 104, 112, 116, 136, 142, 146, 152, 156, 160, 164, 178, 182, 188, 192, 210, 212, 214, 216, 218, 224, 228, 232, 248, 252, 256. St. Hildegard Abbey also contributed some other historic photos: pages 186, 297, 303, 306, 307, 308

Then, we thank the **Libreria Statale** in Lucca, Italy, for the permission to show the visionary images from the 13th-century manuscript of the *Liber Divinorum Operum*: pages 46, 76, 79, 81, 108, 240, 276, 310

For the many other photos from the "Land of Hildegard" we give credit to:

Martina Christ, page 205

Michael Conti, pages 17, 128, 140, 175, 177, 239, 246

Annette Esser, pages 17, 29, 37, 38, 39, 44, 59, 69, 70, 87, 93, 94, 95, 98, 111, 123, 127, 194, 200, 205, 206, 207, 215, 230, 245, 246, 272, 273, 275, 278, 280, 297, 298, 303, 307

Volkhard Loebich, pages 267, 271, 284

Walter Lhotzky, pages 12, 89

Jone van Rees, page 128

Wikimedia Commons, pages 48, 57, 134, 161, 282

About the Author and Contributors

*Annette Esser with her sculpture "Virgin Hildegard"
in the Disibodenberg Chapel in 2018*

Author

Dr. Annette Esser was born in Cologne, Germany, and studied Catholic and Protestant theology, art, psychology, and geography at the universities of Cologne and Münster, Germany, and at Union Theological Seminary in New York, USA. She holds a master of education (1989), master of sacred theology (STM, 1995), doctor of theology (Radboud University, Nijmegen, NL, 2007) and master of visual arts (Mainz Academy of Fine Arts, 2017). She is author and editor of numerous articles and books, especially in the context of the European Society of Women in Theological Research (ESWTR). After having worked as a teacher for many years, she founded the

Scivias Institute for Art and Spirituality in 2008 and has served as its director since (www.scivias-institut.de). In 2017 she initiated the *Hildegard von Bingen Pilgerwanderweg*—the Hildegard Pilgrimage Way.

Contributors

The English edition of *The Hildegard of Bingen Pilgrimage Book* is based on the texts of the 59 tableaux of the Hildegard Way and on the German edition *Pilgerbuch: Hildegard von Bingen Pilgerwanderweg*. Many authors and scholars in the "Land of Hildegard" as well as internationally have supported this whole work by writing texts for the 59 tableaux, by contributing their own new poems, and by proofreading the author's translation.

Margarida Barbal Rodoreda, professor at the *Escola Superior de Música de Catalunya*, Barcelona/Spain, has written about Hildegard's *Symphoniae* and especially about her Marian songs (tableaux 15, 45).

Nathaniel Campbell, adjunct instructor in history at Union College Kentucky, USA, who recently published the first full translation of Hildegard's *Liber Divinorum Operum* (Book of Divine Works), has written the tableau about this (tableau 56).

Ruth van Baak Griffoen, PhD, musicologist, musician, and translator, USA, during her year in Germany, 2019, and while walking with Annette Esser on the whole Hildegard pilgrimage trail, undertook the first proofreading of the English text. She also translated the 1838 Gustav Pfarrius poem, "King Henry's Christmas."

Colleen Keating, Australia, author of *Hildegard of Bingen: A Poetic Journey*, contributed her poem "In Search of Hildegard of Bingen"; on the 2019 international pilgrimage Michael Conti filmed this poem.

Beverly M. Kienzle, PhD, affiliate, Harvard University Standing Committee, USA, and editor of *Hildegard of Bingen: Homilies on the Gospel*, undertook a very careful proofreading of *The Hildegard of Bingen Pilgrimage Book*.

Heike Hildegard Klaft, teacher of Protestant religion and German language in Kirn, Germany, and board member of the Scivias Institute, wrote the text on water and beer (tableau 10).

Nigel J.S. Murray, MA (Oxon), (UK, + in Idar-Oberstein, Germany, 2020), did the first proofreading of all the English texts for the 59 tableaux.

Michael Ptok, MD, president of the Internationale Gesellschaft Hildegard von Bingen, Germany, has compiled the texts on Hildegard's three works, the *Liber Physica*, the *Liber Causae et Curae*, and the *Liber Divinorum Operum* (tableaux 22, 23, 52).

Sr. Philippa Rath, OSB, Germany, has proofread all the texts and questions ("Pilgrim's Reflection") on the 27 meditation tableaux and helped to improve some formulations. She also has contributed her own "Text of the Day" on the history of St. Hildegard's Abbey (stage 10).

Matthias Schmandt, PhD, historian and director of the Bingen Museum am Strom, Germany, has proofread all the 31 information tableaux and also contributed one text on the Hildegard town Bingen itself (tableau 58).

Wilhelm Schweinhard, local vintner in the "Land of Hildegard," Germany, wrote the tableau on wine (tableau 27).

Karen Stock, PhD, geographer, poet, artist, and since 2021 theology and psychology student, Canada, contributed four poems on the great mystic Hildegard.

Debra L. Stoudt, PhD, professor of German at Virginia Tech in Blacksburg, Virginia, USA, and co-editor of *A Companion to Hildegard of Bingen* (Brill, 2014) with Beverly Kienzle, proofread the translation of *The Hildegard of Bingen Pilgrimage Book*, thereby carefully comparing it with the German original text.

Michael Vesper, PhD, historian and director of the Bad Kreuznach Health and Tourism Society (GUT), Germany, has written the important texts on the historic Hildegard sites (tableaux 4, 35, 38, 43, 48).

Eveline Waterboer, PhD, protestant theologian with a recent dissertation on Hildegard of Bingen ("Als das Wort Gottes erklang"), as well as board member of the Scivias Institute, Germany, has contributed the tableau "Hildegard as an Early 'Protestant'" (tableau 11).

Take a Virtual Pilgrimage Along the Hildegard Way!

The author shares a free *Saint Hildegard Speaks* video with the readers of this book.

In these videos, Dr. Annette Esser speaks as Hildegard about many historical subjects along the Hildegard Way in Germany:
- Precious Stones and the Heavenly Jerusalem
- Family and Childhood
- Entrance into the Monastery of St. Disibod
- Teacher Jutta of Sponheim
- Foundation of the Rupertsberg Women's Monastery

The SaintHildegardWay.eu website includes more videos to enjoy. Find upcoming international and local events, a free newsletter sign-up, tour information, and online pilgrimage communities.

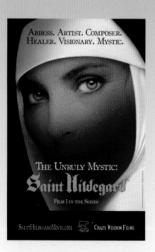

This special ecumenical pilgrimage was created by a pilgrim/filmmaker, Michael M. Conti, creator of *The Unruly Mystic: Saint Hildegard.*

Mr. Conti took the 85-mile "Hildegard Way" in Rhineland-Palatinate, Germany, with Dr. Annette Esser and other pilgrims.

Visit SaintHildegardWay.eu to get access and to learn more about Saint Hildegard.